NED BELL

WITH VALERIE HOWES

L U R E

SUSTAINABLE SEAFOOD RECIPES FROM THE WEST COAST

Vancouver / Berkeley

Cataloguing data is available from
Library and Archives Canada

ISBN 978-1-927958-92-6 (hbk.)

Design by Jessica Sullivan
Photography by Kevin Clark
Food styling by Lawren Moneta
Food styling assistance by Michelle Edgar
Prop styling by Jessica Sullivan
Ceramics by Janaki Larsen
Illustrations by Dale Nigel Goble

Editing by Michelle Meade
Copy editing by Grace Yaginuma
Proofreading by Breanne MacDonald
Recipe editing by Danielle Centoni
Indexing by Iva Cheung

Printed and bound in China by
C&C Offset Printing Co., Ltd.
Distributed in the U.S. by
Publishers Group West

Figure 1 Publishing Inc.
Vancouver BC Canada
www.figure1publishing.com

NOTE: The consumption of raw fish
and seafood, including ceviches and
crudos, poses an increased risk of food-
borne illnesses. To minimize risk, seek
out the best fish and seafood from a
trusted fishmonger who understands
that the fish is to be consumed raw.

My journey, dreams, and happiness—and this book—would not have been possible without the love and support of my family.

I dedicate this book to my amazing wife, Kate; my sons, Fin, Max, and Jet; my mom, Victoria; my dad, Barry, and his wife, Angela; my sister, Freddy, and her family; and my brother, William. You have supported me for many years on wild culinary adventures, not least of all as the best crew ever on the Chefs for Oceans cycle across Canada.

If we focus on community, we can build a deeper understanding of our challenges and opportunities. The 2014 Chefs for Oceans awareness-raising ride across Canada wouldn't have been possible without the support of Linda Morris and the Vancity family. Now, a few short years later, these same amazing people have provided a massive commitment of both financial and community support to this Chefs for Oceans cookbook project, *Lure*. We are indebted to our friends at Vancity. I appreciate and value the opportunity they have given me to share my stories, knowledge, and recipes with a larger audience.

And thank you to the fish for all that you give us! I endeavor each day, through my work as a chef, to honor you and play my part in protecting the lakes, rivers, and oceans where you reside.

NED BELL

To my son and
my heart, Sean.

VALERIE HOWES

"A chef's mission is to create dishes that are, above all, delicious. When the opportunity is also used to communicate a message, the work is complete. *Lure* transports readers to a sea universe and helps them to discover ways of using sustainable seafood. The ocean is a finite resource with infinite possibilities."

ALEX ATALA
Michelin-starred chef and owner of D.O.M.

CONTENTS

RECIPE LIST BY COURSE

RECIPE LIST BY COURSE

FOREWORD

THE INTEGRITY OF A PRODUCT is the foundation on which a chef will build his reputation. It was true when I said this more than twenty years ago, and it is even more relevant now.

Today, my peers continue to laud me for promoting and blazing the trail for high-quality sustainable seafood in Canada, but back in the mid-nineties, I didn't even realize that we had a problem with our watery world. I was frustrated by the fact that no supplier could answer four simple questions: where was this fish caught, when was it caught, how was it caught, and by whom?

So I began doing less business with suppliers and focused on establishing direct relationships with fishermen. It soon became clear that the method of harvesting seafood was the concern. There is a direct correlation between quality and fishing method, and the most sustainable production methods also produce the highest quality.

As Canadians, we are uniquely positioned to lead the world in ocean conservation. We are also capable of creating effective ways to maintain the integrity of our freshwater lakes and rivers. With the longest coastline in the world, and control over one of the largest percentages of freshwater on the planet, I feel we are not only capable but also obligated to lead this initiative.

Chef Ned Bell is one of those leaders who educate and supply us with tools to become part of the solution, not part of the problem. Whether it's his cycling across Canada, his work with the Chefs' Table Society, or his leadership behind Chefs for Oceans, Ned has been working tirelessly to effect change in our industry and, more importantly, he has brought like-minded chefs together to work on sustainable seafood initiatives.

Lure is another example of Ned's commitment, and the next natural step in the evolution of this effort. By bringing sustainable seafood solutions into our homes, Ned has made it easier than ever for families to make healthy, responsible choices.

I hope this cookbook is a great beginning to a series of pivotal sustainable seafood cookbooks. Ned's natural culinary talent—and his many years spent working in some of Canada's most highly regarded kitchens—is felt on every page. I've had the pleasure of cooking alongside Ned at many charity events to promote sustainable seafood. He always respects the integrity of the product and brings creativity to his dishes, exploring ingredients without boundaries or ego. Thank you, Chef.

ROBERT CLARK, 2017

INTRODUCTION

WHEN MY MIDDLE SON, MAX, WAS FOUR, my wife, Kate, and I took him to Maui. As our plane descended through the clouds, and he caught his first glimpse of a turquoise Pacific, he turned to me and said, "Daddy, what's your favorite fish in the ocean that we're allowed to eat?"

We worry all the time as parents about whether we're getting it all wrong, so moments like that are gold. I never lecture my kids about sustainable seafood. But Max was around me enough to listen and absorb, as I chatted with fishers at the wharf, gave cooking demos, and engaged with diners at my restaurant about menu items such as octopus bacon, sea lettuce, and geoduck. He could not yet read or write, but already he understood the importance of making good choices when we take food from the ocean.

Eating seafood responsibly is not about restricting your options; it's about opening your mind (and fridge) to a vast array of fish and shellfish that you might not have considered before. In North America, we're so fixated on the big four—cod, tuna, salmon, and shrimp—that we risk consuming these species to the point of no return.

Fortunately, on the Pacific coast, we're blessed with an abundance of healthy and well-managed wild species, and the commercial fishers are increasingly moving away from practices that put pressure on marine habitat and creatures—and ultimately their livelihood. The ocean is an interdependent ecosystem where it's as important to protect the coral on the seabed as it is to minimize the risks to seabirds and other marine creatures of being entrapped with the target catch. As a father of three, my dream is that we all play our part so future generations can enjoy the same fish and shellfish that we do today. By asking where our seafood comes from and how it was caught—then pulling out our wallets only when we're satisfied with the answers—we have tremendous power to influence the fishing industry.

And that's what this book is all about. I want to simplify your life by sharing delicious recipes, easy techniques, and straightforward sustainability guidelines around Pacific species. These recipes are nutrient-dense and plant-based with a focus on sustainable seafood. I know change can be daunting—it took me close to 20 years to go a hundred percent ocean friendly. But I'm hoping that by sharing my journey, I can help get you there faster. With the guidance of my sustainability partners Ocean Wise,

SeaChoice, Seafood Watch, and Marine Stewardship Council (MSC), I've identified a collection of species that are accessible to most home cooks and relatively straightforward to prepare. They also reflect my West Coast roots, culinary adventures, and passion for the Pacific Ocean. You'll find in these pages sustainable wild Pacific fish and shellfish, as well as responsibly farmed species, which have less impact on the environment, provide a livelihood for fishers from California to Alaska, and help us eat healthy for a better quality of life.

A LIFE-LONG JOURNEY

THE WATER WAS ALWAYS A BIG PART OF MY LIFE. I lived on a farm near Okanagan Lake, in Penticton, BC, until I was two, and was swimming before I could walk. From there we moved to Victoria, where I'd run from our house onto the beach to jump on the bull kelp and make it pop like Bubble Wrap or swing it around my head like helicopter blades. My friends and I scoured rock pools for hermit crabs and tagged along with our fathers on fishing trips. The coastal ecosystem was our tackle box and our playground.

I grew up loving the ocean, but I didn't realize it needed our protection when I was starting out as a young chef. In 1993, I went to culinary school in Vancouver and learned from my incredible first mentors Michel Jacob (Le Crocodile) and Rob Feenie (Lumière). Michel taught me classic technique and the fundamentals of food, and Rob taught me to appreciate local and seasonal produce and how to recognize the hallmarks of quality. But back then when it came to

seafood, nobody was stopping to think about whether any species was being overfished.

In 1997, I moved to Toronto to be an executive chef. There, chefs like Jamie Kennedy and Michael Stadtlander were introducing my generation of chefs to farm-to-table cuisine. Events like Feast of Fields joined the dots between what was on our plates with the farms where it was produced. We knew our farmers by name now. But most of us young chefs in North America still hadn't thought to go meet our fishers.

At that time, we'd scour the menus of our culinary heroes, aspiring to create dishes like theirs. Alongside the heritage beets and Niagara peaches, every menu in the city featured Chilean sea bass and big red tuna. Today, those species are endangered in certain parts of the world. While I introduced some more ocean-friendly Pacific species, such as sablefish and albacore tuna, at that time the concept of sustainable seafood was much more of a foreign concept than, say, organic vegetables and ethically raised meat.

I moved back West and lived in Calgary from 2001 to 2007. I started introducing Pacific species such as lingcod—a favorite to this day—and halibut and BC shrimp onto my menus at Murrieta's West Coast Grill. But they still sat alongside industrially farmed tiger prawns and unsustainable ahi tuna. However, in the early 2000s, I became inspired by one of my Calgarian peers, restaurateur Sal Howell, who began taking her cues from Monterey Bay Aquarium's new Seafood Watch program in choosing the fish and shellfish items for the menus at River Café. At the time it was shocking: "What do

you mean there's no wild salmon this week?" diners asked when they saw their old go-to dishes appear and disappear. But then something surprising happened. People started loving these ever-changing menus, based on what was in season and green-lighted by the folks at Monterey. It meant variety, surprise discoveries, and a more thoughtful approach to dining out—it was a dynamic way to eat.

When Chef Robert Clark, marine biologist Mike McDermid, and the team at the Vancouver Aquarium launched the sustainable seafood-ranking program Ocean Wise in 2004, the restaurant I was running, Redwater Rustic Grille, leapt on board. I created a "Naked Entrees" concept, a choose-your-own-culinary-adventure of sorts by which diners could pick their protein, sauce, and sides from a variety of tasty options to customize their meal. It included many sustainable seafood choices, such as albacore tuna, scallops, and wild Pacific salmon. Signing on with Ocean Wise was the next logical step: their marine biologists pored over scientific studies so we chefs didn't have to. Any menu item with the Ocean Wise seal stamped beside it was a responsible choice, and having that seal all over our menu made us feel like we were doing something bigger than just putting food on plates. Because of its success, I've included a version of Naked Fish in the book (page 33).

I continued to support all things sustainable as chef-owner of the Cabana Grille, in the Okanagan Valley, where I moved to next in 2008. But as the recession hit, most of my energy went to keeping the place afloat. The real opportunity to dive deep came for me in 2011, when an executive chef role opened up at Four Seasons Vancouver. They were rebranding their signature restaurant, YEW, to a seafood concept, and they wanted to build it into something extraordinary. I didn't have a background in international hotel-chain catering, but I had big ideas for the menus based on the core values I'd been developing over the past two decades. I had just one demand when I went for the job: to make YEW a hundred percent Ocean Wise. They took a chance on me, we became the first luxury hotel in Canada to go all in, and I'm forever grateful.

In hotel restaurants, a typical goal is to cater to every traveler by offering a little bit of everything on the menu. At YEW, the direction we chose seemed counterintuitive: we were taking guaranteed performers such as crispy calamari off the menu and replacing them with things like halibut burgers with BC blueberry relish and Dungeness crab tacos. When I told industry folks what we were planning, they looked at me like I was crazy.

Our first menu was a half step in: we got rid of the best-selling shrimp cocktail, which was made with imported tiger prawns, and featured BC spot prawns instead. It was a huge statement, replacing a cheap, industrially farmed, and imported jumbo protein with an expensive, medium-size wild species pulled up in traps by small-boat fishers from local shores. The spotties were a delicacy with a great backstory and ultimately created an even better dining experience.

For our second menu in the spring of 2012, we did a total overhaul, getting creative with interesting ingredients like gooseneck barnacles, humpback shrimp, octopus, sustainably farmed sturgeon, and kelp. Our focus was clean, simple plant-based flavors, superfresh seafood, and ocean-friendly ingredients. Our servers on the front lines learned everything there was to know about the species we were offering and were willing to answer questions and coax people out of their comfort zones. We created what we hoped was an amazing dining experience, and we prayed that consumers would bite.

Thankfully, they did. Customers seemed to love being able to come in and eat something novel and delicious without having to worry if it was ethical too. Notoriously tough *Globe and Mail* food critic Alexandra Gill called us "pitch perfect" and anointed us "the city's new premier seafood restaurant" within the first six months. Things just exploded at that point, and we went from doing a hundred covers to three hundred a night. By the 12-month mark, we could breathe again: the general manager and I could see the concept was working from a business perspective. We grew 40 percent over the next four years, increasing our revenue by a million dollars annually, all the while keeping our costs on budget.

I'd been at YEW for less than a year when I attended a campfire summit of sorts in Nova Scotia, where chefs from across the country had gathered to talk about what food meant in their regions. Many issues came up, but to my surprise, most of my peers—other than those chefs living and working right on the coast—still weren't paying much attention to seafood. I understood then that it was an out-of-sight-out-of-mind issue. We all see what's happening in land-based farming and are quick to kick up a storm if things don't look right. But when it's all happening underwater, you're not confronted with the impact of unsustainable practices and unbridled climate change until one day you wake up and the fish are gone, which is what almost happened in Newfoundland to the cod, and more recently on Desolation Sound, in BC, where there was an oyster and scallop die-off in the billions.

Climate change and overfishing are the two largest threats that our world's oceans face today. I wanted us to go beyond local concerns and start having national, and ultimately international conversations about the future of the fish. Only then could we pull together to protect our oceans, lakes, and rivers. The idea came to me to found Chefs for Oceans. It would be a forum, independent of NGOs, for chefs to discuss and learn about sustainable seafood, and then go back and educate diners in their restaurants by cooking up amazing dishes that would inspire people in turn to cook more ocean-friendly species at home.

I started thinking about making a journey across the country to connect with chefs and diners from coast to coast through collaborative dinners showcasing responsibly harvested fish and shellfish. And I figured that if I did it on a bicycle, the crazy factor might really get them talking. I also wanted to reinforce that connection between personal health and wellness and healthy oceans.

I began fund-raising like mad for a cross-country ride and trained on my bike between restaurant shifts for six months.

I was fully aware that my fitness levels were not where they should be when I set off with my family for St. John's, Newfoundland, on Canada's East Coast. There was incredible stress in the week leading up to the ride. We shipped our support van by train, and it got lost in Montreal, so my brother had to go find it in the shipyards and then drive for 18 hours overnight to St. John's so I could set off, as scheduled, on Canada Day.

Riding 75 to 110 miles a day into headwinds and cooking for a big crowd every other day was demanding. I'd leave the motel alone on my bike at around 5 a.m., and then a few hours later my son, Fin, and my dad would catch up in the support van and join me for a quick roadside breakfast. Then I'd take off again on the bike, riding several hours more to our next destination. This massive challenge was daunting at first, but I enjoyed the time for solitary reflection and soon got into the groove. The changing landscapes, the energy of the people who showed up at our events, and the connections I forged with chefs across the country spurred me on as we planned menus around regional seafood and cooked up a storm together.

On the last day, 50 friends showed up on their bikes in the Fraser Valley. They rode with me for the final stretch into my home city. We had a police escort, and at the Vancouver Aquarium, where the ride ended, a crowd had gathered to cheer us on. It was so emotional. We capped things off with a blowout seafood feast at my restaurant that evening. My bucket was so full by the end: at every event, even though my muscles ached more and more from one city to the next, I'd feel increasingly energized by the growing support for the cause.

After the ride, I didn't touch my bike for at least a month. But I immediately set to work lobbying for a Sustainable Seafood Day on March 18. Living in a country surrounded by three oceans—the Pacific, the Arctic, and the Atlantic—I felt strongly that we needed to be checking in at least once a year for national conversations about their protection. I continue to fight this fight.

AND IN 2016, I REALIZED I WANTED TO TAKE MY ADVOCACY TO THE NEXT LEVEL, and devote more time to the issues. So I made the terrifying move of leaving Four Seasons and accepted a position as the Ocean Wise executive chef and ambassador. In this role, I travel up and down North America, collaborating with chefs I admire and teaching diners how they can have their (sustainable) crab cake and eat it, too. (There's a recipe for crab cakes on page 116, by the way.) Being in daily contact with the Ocean Wise team of marine biologists and experts allows me to have my own questions answered immediately all day long. It's like doing a masters in sustainable seafood—only without the late-night cramming and tuition fees.

I'm a West Coast boy, born and raised, and I look out to the Pacific every day on my commute through Stanley Park. I love that ocean with a passion. Having gone on as a chef to discover its bounty from California to Alaska, I'm excited about getting *you* excited about some of the beautiful sustainable seafood products it has to offer.

DIVING
DEEP

GLOBALLY INSPIRED, LOCALLY CREATED

MOST OF THE RECIPES YOU FIND IN THESE PAGES reflect the kind of dishes I'd make for my family at home at the end of a long day: I'm saving the cheffy touches for another time. They are fast and the flavors are approachable, so they won't scare off your kids if seafood is new to them. In these pages, you'll find fish burgers, chowders, and sandwiches—the types of dishes that fill bellies, soothe souls, and get happy dinner-table conversation flowing on a weeknight. I've also thrown in some elegant (albeit simple-to-execute) dinner-party options, such as crudo, ceviche, and paella.

Having learned to cook in multicultural cities with diverse influences, I focus on local ingredients but play with global flavors. And since I'm tired of going to my local grocery store and seeing that the vast majority of the protein choices are meat, I've not included as much as an ounce of steak or a strip of pork-based bacon in these recipes. Let's all ask our local store managers for more ocean-friendly seafood choices—that's how we bring about change.

As a cyclist, runner, and the father of three active boys, I pay attention to what I put in my body, so most of the recipes in this book are plant-forward. Sometimes the seafood serves as no more than a garnish, and if we can get used to eating this way rather than dropping an eight-ounce chunk of protein on our plates each time, we can benefit from the healthy oils and rich nutrients that seafood delivers without depleting the oceans of every last fish.

My challenge to you now is to commit to trying one new recipe a week and one new species a month—that makes for 52 sustainable seafood meals and 12 new species in a year. I wish you well as you embark on your wild Pacific adventure!

HOW TO USE THIS BOOK

I'VE IDENTIFIED DELICIOUS AND HEALTHY fish and shellfish species available off the Pacific coast that can be caught or farmed responsibly with minimal impact on the environment. These are profiled in the book (beginning on page 176), so you can discover what I love about them, how they are sustainable, and how best to prepare them.

Lure is as much about a healthy and inspired diet as it is about a healthy ocean—it's also a collection of some of my favorite recipes. This book includes my take on classics such as spaghetti with clams (page 113), fish and chips (page 43), and planked wild salmon (page 85), as well as some unexpected surprises. As a West Coast boy, I like to make the most of regional bounty. I've discovered that incredible depths of flavor can be achieved by preparing ocean edibles with nontraditional ingredients such as vanilla or stone fruit—and I'm asking you to trust me on the surprise element in this recipe: (Sea)Weed Brownies (page 175). The dishes in this book are organized into four categories: white fish, fatty fish, shellfish, and sea greens.

And finally, Back to Basics on page 24 features essential information for buying, storing, and preparing fish.

MAKING WAVES

We have more choice now than we've ever had—the things we buy, the services we use, the food we eat. This can be a great thing, but there's often a cost and it's not always about money.

When we choose food that's been transported thousands of miles or produced in ways that damage the environment or the ecosystem, we pay the price in terms of less vibrant communities and damaged or depleted resources.

We have immense power both as individuals and as organizations to support local, sustainable food systems. As a values-based financial institution, Vancity believes that where we invest our members' money can make a real difference. We support businesses, not-for-profit organizations, and projects that focus on local and organic food because it builds a more resilient local economy and healthier communities.

We are proud to build partnerships with leaders in food sustainability, and Ned Bell is a perfect example. His passion for sustainable seafood has inspired professional chefs and home cooks alike to be more thoughtful in their seafood choices. It's fitting that many of the organizations we support are featured in *Lure*: community partners such as Skipper Otto, Organic Ocean, SeaChoice, and Ocean Wise are all playing their parts to ensure we have healthy oceans for generations to come.

We're so lucky to live in a region with a thriving local food sector and, of course, an ocean that supplies us with fresh, sustainable, and delicious food options. Thanks to Ned's unrivaled expertise and enthusiasm, you'll find many of them in this book. Bon appétit!

TAMARA VROOMAN
President and CEO, Vancity Credit Union

"Chef Ned Bell is a tireless advocate for our oceans and this cookbook is a beautiful culmination of his efforts to date. *Lure* is sure to inspire another generation of ocean ambassadors."

DR. JOHN NIGHTINGALE
CEO of Vancouver Aquarium

BACK TO BASICS

What better way to take advantage of the abundance of fish along our coastlines than to prepare it at home—especially when it's this easy to find and cook? Here are the essentials for buying, preparing, and cooking.

THE OCEAN GUARDIANS

Let me be the first to admit that when it comes to seafood, keeping track of what's sustainable can be a challenge. With meat or vegetables, you can be pretty sure that local + organic = an excellent choice. With fish, you need to factor in the species, where it was caught, and how it was raised and harvested—harvesting methods vary in their impact on the environment and untargeted species. And the status of any fish or shellfish may change from one year to the next, as its population rises and falls and as fisheries modify their management strategies and harvesting techniques.

Thankfully, there are NGOs out there doing great work to keep track of what's what and presenting it to us consumers in simple and bang-up-to-date forms, via their apps and websites. They don't agree on everything, but the debate is healthy, and I try to walk a middle ground. You can download your favorite app onto your smartphone and have information about hundreds of species at your fingertips as you shop and dine out, and never have to worry again about whether a fish is OK to eat. Here are some of my favorites.

SEAFOOD WATCH

Monterey Bay Aquarium, in California, launched their game-changing sustainable seafood program, Seafood Watch, in 1999. Their guides and app indicate which seafood items are "Best Choices" or "Good Alternatives" and which to "Avoid."

seafoodwatch.org

SEACHOICE

The Canadian cousin of Monterey Bay Aquarium's Seafood Watch, SeaChoice ensures transparency and traceability along the supply chain, helps to reduce seafood misrepresentation through better labeling laws, and provides tools to Canadian retailers to improve their sustainable seafood commitments.

seachoice.org

OCEAN WISE

Vancouver Aquarium's Ocean Wise sustainable seafood program was devised to make dining out easier and encourage chefs to put more sustainable choices on menus. Participating restaurants and fishmongers put the Ocean Wise symbol beside approved fish and shellfish items. The Ocean Wise app is useful for grocery shopping too: it presents the basic facts around sustainability species by species.

ocean.org/seafood

MARINE STEWARDSHIP COUNCIL (MSC)

A global nonprofit organization, MSC makes it easy to choose seafood that is certified sustainable, traceable, and wild. It works together with fisheries and companies to effect change, address food fraud, and protect our last major food source that is truly wild. Look for the blue MSC label on seafood at grocery stores, fishmongers, and restaurants.

msc.org

Monterey Bay Aquarium

SEAFOOD SEASONALITY

AVAILABLE YEAR ROUND

SEA GREENS
DULSE
KELP
SEA ASPARAGUS

SHELLFISH
CLAMS
GEODUCK
MUSSELS
OCTOPUS
OYSTERS
SCALLOPS
SEA URCHIN
SQUID

WHITE FISH
ARCTIC CHAR
PACIFIC COD
ROCKFISH
SKATE
STURGEON

FATTY FISH
KUTERRA
FARMED
SALMON
SABLEFISH
STEELHEAD

SEASONAL SEAFOOD

CRAB ⬤ [May–Oct]

SHRIMP ⬤ [May–Nov]

HALIBUT ⬤ [Mar–Oct]

LINGCOD ⬤ [Apr–Nov]

SALMON ⬤ [May–Oct]

SARDINES ⬤ [Jun–Feb]

TUNA ⬤ [May–Nov]

● HOW TO BUY FISH AND SHELLFISH

WHEN BUYING MEAT, most people will trust that it's fresh, but with seafood you need to take a more multisensory approach. Look for firm flesh, clear eyes, and pink gills as signs of freshness. Fresh fish should smell of the sea. Don't turn your nose up at frozen—because many fishers are out at sea for days at a time, and these fish are frozen on the boat, they're often the freshest option. And if the idea of deboning and portioning fish fills you with fear, just ask your fish vendor to do it for you—it's their job and they likely take great pride in doing it right.

When you're buying fresh shellfish, they should have a bright and briny and almost odorless smell. Mussels, clams, and oysters should have their shells tightly shut. If you see them just a touch open, do the tap test to see if they're alive and healthy: when you tap the tip of the shells together, they should shut tight; if they spring back open, the shellfish has already died and should be discarded. Shrimp, lobster, and crab are best bought in the shell. Octopus are difficult to wrangle live and can require a huge cooking pot, so I recommend that you buy their legs frozen to prepare at home. You can also buy quality shrimp in the freezer section—they're flash frozen right on the boat, so they're superfresh.

● HOW TO STORE FISH

FRESH SEAFOOD is best cooked and enjoyed soon after you bring it home. Try to use it the same day or the day after you buy it, and store in the coldest part of the fridge, at the back. If buying vacuum-packed frozen fish that's not in season (like salmon, halibut, and lingcod), remember to use it before the season starts up again.

With live shellfish, don't tie a knot in the plastic bag as oxygen has to get in. And don't fill the bag with ice—as it melts into fresh water, these saltwater dwellers will drown.

HOW TO MAKE SUSTAINABLE CHOICES

Get to know your fishmonger.
By asking what's freshest and in season, you can stick to the best seafood options from local waters.

Just ask, "Is this fish sustainable?"
If your server or fish retailer doesn't know, you probably have your answer. Next, ask where it's from, how it's harvested, and if it's certified.

Download a sustainable seafood app onto your smartphone for instant info on every species.
Ocean Wise, Seafood Watch, MSC, and SeaChoice all have great smartphone tools.

Look for ecolabels such as Ocean Wise and MSC at the fish counter.
You may also come across tags, barcodes, or QR codes that you can scan with your smartphone, or a ThisFish code to punch into the website thisfish.info. These are designed to support traceability, allowing you to instantly discover who caught the fish, where, when, and how.

Join a community-supported fisheries (CSF) program.
You'll buy shares at the start of the season for regular deliveries of traceable and affordable seafood caught by local fishers.

Eat lower on the food chain.
Consuming small fish such as sardines, anchovies, mackerel, and herring typically has less impact than eating big predator fish. You still need to check your sustainability app nonetheless, as any species can end up endangered as food trends, environmental factors, and management strategies change.

When on the Pacific, eat Pacific.
Supporting local fishers and economies is an often-overlooked aspect of sustainability.

Experiment with seaweed.
It's a superfood, and wild seaweed and marine plant aquaculture can actually heal ocean environments.

When choosing fresh seafood, eat with the seasons.
You know it's not ideal to eat imported strawberries in winter, and the same goes for off-season fresh wild fish species, which have to be shipped from afar.

Don't be afraid of the deep freeze.
Fresh is best, but properly thawed frozen fish is still delicious, and freezing allows us to enjoy locally caught species out of season.

Favor filter feeders.
Shellfish such as oysters, mussels, and clams clean the ocean and stimulate marine diversity.

Try something new.
There's more in our oceans, lakes, and rivers than you think. To keep the pressure off our most popular species, ask your fish vendor what else they have in store. Sea urchins, anyone?

Don't treat fish like steak.
You don't need a 10-ounce slab of protein—make smaller portions of high-quality and sustainable fish the supporting cast in plant-forward dishes.

HOW TO COOK FISH

People are often surprised by how easy it is to prepare fish: it requires only a few choice tools and minimal equipment and cooking time. Just keep in mind that the methods and cooking times in this book may need slight adjustments depending on the species and the size of your fish pieces. Love, care, and attention will go a long way! My favorite methods range from pan-frying to poaching to curing ceviche-style.

PAN-FRYING

BEST FOR

all fish; some of my favorites to pan-fry are wild salmon, arctic char, and halibut

TOOLS: Invest in a cast-iron or heavy-duty stainless-steel pan that you can put right into the oven, if required. These heavy-bottomed pans hold the heat well and distribute it evenly (if the bottom is too thin, it's easy to burn your fish). The bigger your spatula the better for keeping fish intact when you flip it.

PREP: Start with a cleaned fish that you've patted dry with paper towels. Whenever possible, I fry the fish with the skin on—this helps hold in the moisture and makes the skin crisp up nicely to add interesting texture to your dish. Season the fish on both sides with salt and pepper.

METHOD: Heat canola, olive, or vegetable oil in the pan over medium-high heat until the oil is almost smoking but not scorching. This temperature at the start gives the fish a nice sear and, in most cases, cooks the fish through to the middle. For fillets with the skin on, lay the fish skin side down in the pan; you want a golden-brown caramelization and crispy edges. Be sure not to crowd the pan as the temperature will drop and create too much steam to properly sear the fish. If you're working with a particularly thick piece of fish or a sturdier species, you may need to pop it into a 375°F to 425°F oven (adjust according to the density and thickness of the fish) for a few minutes, to make sure the middle's cooked and the outside is not too tough.

TIMING: The cooking time depends on the density and thickness of the fish, so adjust these recommendations accordingly for extrathick or thin pieces. Delicate species such as rainbow trout need about 2 minutes each side; species that are in between delicate and sturdy, such as wild salmon, need about 3 minutes each side; and more sturdy species, such as halibut, need 3 to 4 minutes each side.

TOOLS: A casserole dish, roasting tray, or rimmed baking sheet works great for baking fish—something deep enough to contain any juices. You can also wrap your fish with parchment paper and bake it *en papillote*. This traps the juices and essentially cooks the fish in its own steam.

PREP: Clean your fish (skin on or off), pat it dry, and either marinate it for up to 15 minutes or drizzle it with oil just before baking. Add a squeeze of citrus (such as lemon, lime, orange, or even grapefruit), season with sea salt and coarsely ground black pepper, and toss in your herbs of choice (I prefer fresh parsley, dill, thyme, chervil, and chives). You can also bake with citrus slices laid on top.

If you're baking *en papillote*, cut a heart shape from parchment paper large enough to contain the fish when folded in half. Arrange your favorite aromatic ingredients (such as chopped shallots, sliced garlic, finely chopped peppers, and citrus slices) in the paper, add the fish, and fold the edges in small overlapping folds starting at the top of the heart, and then twisting the bottom at the end to create a sealed pouch. Be careful not to overstuff so that there's room for the steam to circulate inside during baking.

METHOD: Bake the fish in a preheated oven at a temperature of 375°F to 425°F, adjusting the heat and oven time according to the density and thickness of the fish.

TIMING: A 5-ounce portion of fish will take 7 to 9 minutes to bake. You will need more heat and time if you're baking your fish alongside a bunch of other ingredients in the pan. And whole fish will need almost twice as long as smaller fillets. Test for doneness by carefully inserting a skewer into the fish. If there's any resistance, it needs more time. Alternatively, gently pinch the fish with your index finger and thumb. If it feels firm but tender, it's cooked.

BAKING

BEST FOR
meaty, fatty fish such as salmon and sablefish

TOOLS: Whole fish can be grilled directly on a clean BBQ and fillets in a grill pan (which will create a barrier between the heat source and the fish).

PREP: Trim off any ragged edges and pat-dry the fish. Brush it with olive, vegetable, or canola oil and season it with salt and pepper. Alternatively, use a simple marinade or dry rub. Avoid leaving excess marinade on the fish to prevent flare-ups.

METHOD: Put your fish on the preheated grill at a medium-high heat and wait at least 2 to 3 minutes before moving or flipping it (so that it doesn't stick and the char lines are clean). A gas BBQ will get the job done, but for extra layers of flavor, use charcoal or smoky-flavored wood such as apple or cedar.

TIMING: The general rule for cooking fish is 5 to 6 minutes per inch of thickness. Test for doneness by carefully inserting a thin skewer into the fish. If there's any resistance, it needs more time. Alternatively, gently pinch the fish with your index finger and thumb. If it feels firm but tender, it's cooked.

GRILLING

BEST FOR
fatty and/or sturdy fish (such as wild salmon and lingcod) and octopus

POACHING

BEST FOR
any fish

TOOLS: You'll need a saucepan large enough for the fish portion to lie flat inside. There are special fish poaching pans out there with a long slim form to better accommodate whole fish—not mandatory but a nice-to-have.

PREP: Simply clean the fish under cold running water.

METHOD: Poaching is a means of gently steaming fish in stock or water with aromatics—celery, fennel bulb, shallots, garlic, bay leaves, and fresh thyme. You can also do a confit (cooking slowly over a long period of time in fat or oil). Bring the stock or water up to a simmer over medium heat, and gently lay the fish in the pan. Use just enough liquid to cover the top of the fish.

TIMING: The average fish portion takes about 6 minutes to poach. The fish is cooked when some of the natural fats start to show on the surface of the fish.

STEAMING

BEST FOR
shellfish, particularly mussels and clams

TOOLS: A large pot with a decent surface area prevents the shellfish from overcrowding and ensures enough space for the mussels to open. Avoid tall stockpots, which will cook the shellfish at the bottom first and leave the top layer underdone.

PREP: Carefully rinse the shellfish under cold water. Remove the beard of a mussel by pinching the end between your thumb and index finger and firmly tugging it out. Store-bought fresh clams just need to be rinsed well under cold running water for about 5 minutes.

METHOD: In a shallow pot, sauté chopped garlic, fennel bulb, and shallots in olive oil or butter; add the shellfish, and then pour in apple juice, white wine, or beer to deglaze. Use 1 cup of liquid for every 3 to 5 pounds of shellfish. (Mussels need less than clams.) Add the shellfish and stir. Cover the pot with a lid and cook the shellfish until they open.

TIMING: 2 to 3 minutes cooking time—shellfish are the ultimate fast food!

CEVICHE

BEST FOR
albacore tuna, scallops, spot prawns, and white fish

TOOLS: Use a nonreactive glass or ceramic bowl (metal can leave a metallic aftertaste).

PREP: Pat-dry ultrafresh sashimi-grade fish. Trim off the ragged edges to create consistent pieces, ½- to ¼-inch cubes or slices, for uniform marinating.

METHOD: Ceviche requires a wet marinade with a one-to-one ratio of citrus juice to oil (a little less citrus if you're using lemon and lime as it's more acidic than, say, orange or grapefruit). The fish should be almost completely submerged in this liquid.

TIMING: The longer the fish marinates, the more it cooks—especially with sharper citrus such as lemon or lime. Marinate for 3 to 5 minutes (and up to 10 minutes maximum, depending on the density of the fish) before serving.

NAKED FISH

"Naked Fish" is my unique approach to building a recipe. You can create a bespoke dish just by choosing the fish, sauce, carb, and vegetable—there are thousands of possible outcomes. It's a fun and delicious way to explore new and exciting flavor combinations.

For special occasions, a large spread with the various components makes a fantastic presentation and provides friends and family with a unique and healthy dining experience.

1+ FISH	**2+** METHOD (PAGES 30 TO 32)	**3+** SAUCE (PAGES 34 TO 35)	**4+** CARB	**5** VEGETABLE
• Wild salmon	• Pan-frying	• Honey Lemon Vinaigrette	• Crushed new potatoes	• Steamed green beans
• Halibut	• Baking	• Vanilla Lime Vinaigrette	• Mashed golden potatoes	• Grilled asparagus
• Tuna	• Grilling	• Curry Vanilla Vinaigrette	• Roasted spuds or sweet potatoes	• Roasted and marinated bell peppers
• Shrimp	• Poaching	• Grain-Mustard Maple Vinaigrette	• Quinoa	• Caramelized cauliflower and broccoli
• Spot prawns	• Ceviche	• Pickled Ginger Vinaigrette	• Brown or wild rice	• Roasted root vegetables such as beets, parsnips, or celery root
• Scallops		• Olive Oil Mayonnaise	• Lentils	
• Sablefish		• Lime Mayonnaise	• Chickpeas	• Sautéed kale, Swiss chard, and beet greens
		• Fennel Mayonnaise	• Assorted beans or legumes	
		• Lemon Aioli	• Wheatberries	
		• Citrus Butter	• Farro	
		• Honey, Ginger, and Seaweed Butter		
		• Beurre Blanc		
		• Nectarine BBQ Sauce		

SAUCES

I keep an arsenal of vinaigrettes, compound butters, and mayos in the fridge. As a chef and a parent of young children, sometimes I need to create quick and delicious meals that satisfy appetites. These incredibly versatile sauces make a great impact with little effort: you simply prepare them in advance, and then prepare your fish or seafood in your favorite manner, and you have an incredible meal in 20-some minutes. Naked Fish on page 33 offers a few ways of using these sauces on fish or shellfish. A great blender is ideal for these recipes—I swear by my Vitamix.

I always keep a squeeze bottle of what I call Chef's Juice by the stove—two parts olive oil and one part lemon juice—and I use it to finish many of my dishes. Just mix together and squeeze on almost any dish to add a hit of acidity and flavor-boosting healthy fats.

CLASSIC SAUCES

CHEF'S JUICE
2 parts extra-virgin olive oil
1 part lemon juice

BEURRE BLANC
½ cup white wine
½ cup white wine vinegar
1 shallot, finely chopped
1 bay leaf
¼ tsp salt
1 cup (2 sticks) chilled unsalted butter, cut into 1-inch cubes
2 Tbsp sturgeon or salmon caviar (optional)
1 Tbsp finely chopped fresh chives

NECTARINE BBQ SAUCE
2 Tbsp canola oil
1 shallot, chopped
1 yellow, orange, or red bell pepper, seeded and chopped
1 tsp sea salt
1 tsp coarsely ground black pepper
2 to 3 lb ripe nectarines, apricots, or peaches, pitted and chopped into ¼-inch pieces
½ cup water
½ cup honey or maple syrup
½ cup verjus, white wine vinegar, or white balsamic
1 to 2 canned chipotle peppers, chopped

While I've featured some of my favorite sauces throughout the book, these two classics can elevate any family-style seafood dish. I love *beurre blanc* (butter sauce) during winter months, occasionally with caviar added for extra luxury. The BBQ sauce is a taste of summer. They can be stored up to 2 weeks in the refrigerator. Makes 2 cups.

BEURRE BLANC Combine the white wine, vinegar, shallots, bay leaf, and salt in a saucepan and bring to a boil over high heat. Reduce to medium heat and simmer for 5 minutes or until it's reduced to one-quarter of the original volume. Strain through a fine-mesh sieve into a small saucepan, heat over medium-low heat, and whisk in the butter, one cube at a time. This takes a while to do properly to prevent the sauce from splitting—the key is to maintain a warm (not hot, not cold) temperature. Stir in the caviar, if using, and chives.

NECTARINE BBQ SAUCE Heat the oil in a medium saucepan over medium heat, add the shallots and peppers, and sauté for 10 minutes or until tender. Season with the salt and pepper, add the remaining ingredients, and cook for 20 minutes or until the nectarines are tender. Transfer the mixture to a blender or food processor and puree until smooth. Adjust seasoning to taste.

VINAIGRETTES

In a medium bowl, combine all the ingredients but the oil(s) and whisk until well blended. While whisking, slowly drizzle the oil in a thin steady stream until incorporated and the mixture is emulsified. Adjust seasoning to taste. (Alternatively, you can do this with an immersion blender or in a blender or small food processor.) They can be stored for up to 2 weeks in the refrigerator. Makes about 1¼ cups.

HONEY LEMON VINAIGRETTE
Zest and juice of 1 lemon
1½ Tbsp Dijon mustard
1 Tbsp honey
½ tsp sea salt
½ cup canola oil
½ cup extra-virgin olive oil

VANILLA LIME VINAIGRETTE
Zest and juice of 1 lime
Scraped seeds of ½ vanilla bean
1½ Tbsp Dijon mustard
1 Tbsp honey
½ tsp sea salt
1 cup canola oil

CURRY VANILLA VINAIGRETTE
½ Tbsp Dijon mustard
1 Tbsp Indian or Thai curry paste
Juice of 1 lemon
Scraped seeds of ½ vanilla bean
½ tsp sea salt
1 cup canola oil

GRAIN-MUSTARD MAPLE VINAIGRETTE
2 Tbsp red wine vinegar
1½ Tbsp whole grain mustard
1 Tbsp maple syrup
¼ tsp sea salt
½ cup canola oil
½ cup extra-virgin olive oil

PICKLED GINGER VINAIGRETTE
1½ Tbsp pickled ginger juice
1 Tbsp pickled ginger
1 Tbsp umeboshi plum paste
1 Tbsp Dijon mustard
1 Tbsp honey
¼ tsp sea salt
1 cup canola oil

MAYONNAISE + AIOLIS

In a blender, food processor, or the bowl of a stand mixer fitted with the whisk attachment, combine the eggs, yolks (if called for), and mustard, and blend until well mixed. With the machine running, gradually add the oil(s) in a thin, steady stream until thick and creamy. (You can also do this with just a bowl and a whisk or an immersion blender.) Add the remaining ingredients, and then adjust seasoning to taste. The mayonnaise can be stored for up to 3 days in the refrigerator. Makes about 1½ cups.

OLIVE OIL MAYONNAISE
1 egg
1 egg yolk
1½ Tbsp Dijon mustard
¾ cup extra-virgin olive oil
¼ cup canola oil
Zest and juice of 1 lime or lemon
½ tsp sea salt

LEMON AIOLI
1 egg
1 egg yolk
1½ Tbsp Dijon mustard
¾ cup extra-virgin olive oil
¼ cup canola oil
Zest and juice of 1½ lemons
½ tsp finely chopped garlic
½ tsp sea salt

LIME MAYONNAISE
1 egg
1 egg yolk
1½ Tbsp Dijon mustard
1 cup canola oil
Zest and juice of 2 limes
1½ Tbsp Sriracha (optional)
½ tsp sea salt

FENNEL MAYONNAISE
3 eggs
1 Tbsp Dijon mustard
1 cup canola oil
Zest and juice of 1 lime
1 tsp sea salt

1 Tbsp chopped fennel fronds
1 Tbsp finely chopped fennel bulb

NOTE
You can either just mix in the fennel bulb by hand, or puree it with the rest of the ingredients.

COMPOUND BUTTERS

Butters can be flavored with everything from fresh herbs to tropical fruits and make a great addition to any fish (or vegetables!). Combine the ingredients together in a bowl and mix well. Transfer the butter to a piece of plastic wrap, and then shape and roll it into a 2-inch-diameter log. Chill in the refrigerator. It can be stored up to 5 days in the refrigerator or 6 months in the freezer. Makes about 1¼ cups.

CITRUS BUTTER
1 cup (2 sticks) salted butter, softened
Zest of 2 lemons
½ Tbsp finely chopped shallots
½ Tbsp finely chopped fresh chives

HONEY, GINGER, AND SEAWEED BUTTER
1 cup (2 sticks) unsalted butter, softened
½ Tbsp grated fresh ginger
¼ cup finely chopped fresh dulse and kelp (or use dried but soak in cold water for several minutes before chopping)

2 tsp whole grain mustard
4 tsp honey
½ Tbsp sea salt
¾ tsp coarsely ground black pepper

CHAR • 39—41

[profile 181]

WHITE FISH

COD • 43—45

[profile 185]

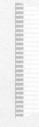

HALIBUT • 46—52

[profile 191]

LINGCOD • 53—56

[profile 193]

ROCKFISH • 57—60

[profile 201]

SKATE • 61—63

[profile 221]

STURGEON • 64—67

[profile 225]

WHITE FISH

FROM LIGHT AND FLAKY lingcod to firm and buttery sablefish, white fish share a clean and relatively simple flavor profile. A boneless four- to five-ounce piece of any white fish makes the perfect blank canvas for building a dish most people will be enthusiastic to try.

White fish such as Pacific cod, rockfish, lingcod, and sturgeon have a more classic fish shape—cylindrical body with an eye peering out from either side of their head. (As a rule of thumb, the round species, such as cod, sturgeon, and lingcod, are higher in fat.) On the other hand, white fish such as halibut and big skate live on the ocean floor and look like they've been run over by a steamroller. Halibut is indeed a funny-looking creature in its natural state—an enormous diamond with asymmetrical googly eyes and an off-kilter grin. Because they while away their days doing as little as possible, their flesh has less muscle tone and is typically lighter and easier to digest. Halibut has been the gateway fish for my youngest sons Max and Jet. Pearly fleshed, satisfyingly steak-like, yet subtle in flavor, it's easy to love cooked—especially when you bring ketchup and hand-cut fries into the equation.

White fish respond well to fresh herbs, butter, and citrus. A classic French sauce makes a nice treat, but you could stop at a knob of butter and a squeeze of lemon on your cod or char, and you'd be sitting down to eat something quite perfect. Vegetables with a natural sweetness and mildness— from spring peas to fennel to squash—make balanced complements. And we're blessed with all kinds of wonderful indigenous fruits on the West Coast that bring out the best in them too: I'm thinking peaches, plums, apples, and pears—go raid an orchard!

I suggest you flip straight to the halibut burger in this chapter (page 46). With its gorgeous deep-purple blueberry relish, this dish was a best seller at YEW. Another great one to try is the classic fish and chips with Pacific cod on page 43—perfection! And if you're feeling adventurous, explore the deep and fragrant spiced flavors and interesting textures of the pan-seared skate with its shiitake mushroom, sake, and ginger broth and sweet-and-spicy cashews (page 63).

This soulful dish warms you up from the inside. The oat-and-barley porridge make for a restorative risotto of sorts; the brown butter lends richness; and a lashing of birch syrup—mahogany nectar whose distinctive flavor lies somewhere on the spectrum between maple syrup and molasses—brings it all together.

ARCTIC CHAR WITH OAT AND BARLEY PORRIDGE, CARROTS, BROWN BUTTER, AND BIRCH SYRUP

OAT AND BARLEY PORRIDGE Combine the barley, water, shallots, bay leaf, and thyme in a medium saucepan, and cook, covered, over medium heat for 15 minutes. Add the oats and cook for another 7 to 9 minutes or until the barley is tender but toothsome.

Reduce the heat to medium-low and cook for another 10 to 12 minutes, stirring continuously, until the water is completely absorbed and the porridge is creamy. (The heat combined with the constant stirring will create the perfect consistency.) Remove the thyme and bay leaf, stir in the butter, and season with salt and pepper.

PAN-SEARED CARROTS Heat the oil in a large, heavy-bottomed skillet over medium-high heat, add the carrots, and sear for 5 minutes or until lightly caramelized. Turn over and sear for another 5 minutes or until browned and the carrots are tender. Season with salt and black pepper. (Alternatively, roast the carrots in a 425°F oven for 20 minutes or until golden brown and tender.)

BROWN BUTTER Melt the butter in a small saucepan over low heat and gently simmer for 5 minutes or until the milk solids turn golden brown and fall to the bottom of the pan. Transfer to a small bowl.

ARCTIC CHAR Preheat the oven to 400°F and line a baking sheet with aluminum foil.

Season the fish with salt and pepper, place it on the baking sheet skin side down, and bake for 5 minutes. Flip the fish over, and bake for another 2 to 5 minutes or until opaque almost all the way through. Remove the fish from the oven and peel off the skin. (It should peel off easily when the fish is perfectly cooked.)

Using a vegetable peeler, shave the carrots lengthwise to create long, thin ribbons.

To assemble the dish, ladle the porridge into 4 individual bowls, place the seared carrots on top, and add the char. Garnish with the carrot ribbons, and then drizzle over 1 to 2 tablespoons of brown butter and 1 teaspoon of birch syrup.

CHEF'S NOTES: Pearl barley has been milled to remove the hull, bran, and endosperm of the grain. It's light in color, cooks quickly, and releases its starch during cooking, resulting in creamy, tender grains.

When you buy the arctic char, have your fishmonger leave the skin on, but do remove the pin bones. You'll peel off the skin after baking the fish once it has worked its magic in keeping the flesh moist and tender.

Birch syrup comes from the sap of birch trees and is produced in the same way as maple syrup. However, it's far less sweet and has a more complex flavor. Look for it at gourmet markets or through online retailers.

OAT AND BARLEY PORRIDGE
1 cup pearl barley (see Notes)
1¼ quarts water
½ shallot, finely chopped
1 small bay leaf
1 small sprig thyme
½ cup old-fashioned (rolled) oats or steel-cut oats
1½ tsp unsalted butter
Sea salt and coarsely ground black pepper

PAN-SEARED CARROTS
2 Tbsp olive oil
1 lb medium carrots, sliced in half lengthwise (and crosswise if they are long)
Sea salt and coarsely ground black pepper

BROWN BUTTER
½ cup (1 stick) unsalted butter

ARCTIC CHAR
4 (4 to 5 oz) skin-on arctic char fillets
Sea salt and coarsely ground black pepper
2 carrots, for garnish
4 tsp birch syrup, to serve (see Notes)

The marriage between earthy root vegetables and fragrant vanilla makes for an unlikely coupling, but it works. And the vinaigrette is especially delicious with rich arctic char, which is very similar to salmon. This rustic dish works best with lentils that hold their shape well when cooked, such as Laird, beluga, or Le Puy lentils. If you end up with large parsnips, be sure to remove the woody cores.

SERVES 4

PAN-SEARED ARCTIC CHAR WITH LENTILS, PARSNIPS, AND VANILLA VINAIGRETTE

VANILLA VINAIGRETTE Combine the vinegar, vanilla, honey, mustard, and salt in a small bowl. While whisking, slowly drizzle the oil in a thin steady stream until incorporated and the mixture is emulsified. Adjust seasoning to taste. (Alternatively, you can do this with an immersion blender or in a blender or small food processor.) Can be made ahead of time; will keep refrigerated for up to 2 weeks.

ROASTED PARSNIPS Preheat the oven to 400°F. Combine the parsnips and olive oil in a large bowl, toss, and season with salt and pepper. Transfer to a baking sheet and roast for 20 to 30 minutes, stirring halfway through, until golden brown, tender, and slightly caramelized.

PARSNIP PUREE Bring a large pot of water to a boil over high heat. Salt generously and add the parsnips. Boil for about 15 minutes, until very tender. Drain, transfer to a blender or food processor, and add the butter or oil. Puree until smooth. Season with salt and pepper to taste.

LENTILS In a large saucepan, combine the lentils, water, garlic, bay leaves, and thyme. Bring to a boil over high heat, then reduce to low heat and cover. Simmer for 25 minutes or until tender. Drain off any excess water.

Remove and discard the garlic, bay leaves, and thyme. Season with salt and pepper to taste. (Can be made several days ahead and refrigerated. Reheat before serving.)

ARCTIC CHAR Preheat the oven to 400°F. Use paper towels to pat-dry the fish and season with salt and pepper. Heat the oil in a heavy-bottomed, ovenproof skillet over medium-high heat until almost smoking. Carefully lay the fish in the pan skin side down. (If necessary, cook the fish in batches to prevent overcrowding, which will keep the fish from caramelizing properly.) Reduce the heat to medium and cook for 1 minute, or until a golden crust forms on the skin. Flip the fillets over and cook for another 2 to 3 minutes, until browned. Place the pan in the oven and roast for 3 to 4 minutes, or until the fish is opaque in the center and flakes easily.

Remove from the oven and add the butter to the pan. Allow it to melt while you squeeze the lemon over the fish. Use a spoon to baste each fillet with the buttery juices for about 1 minute. Transfer to a plate.

To assemble, put the fish on a platter or individual plates, add the pureed and roasted parsnips, and spoon over the warm lentils. Top with the vinaigrette and garnish with parsley and hazelnuts. Serve.

VANILLA VINAIGRETTE
2 Tbsp white wine vinegar
¼ vanilla bean, split lengthwise and seeds scraped
1½ tsp honey
2 tsp Dijon mustard
¼ tsp sea salt
½ cup canola oil

ROASTED PARSNIPS
4 parsnips, peeled and cut into various sizes
1 Tbsp olive oil
Sea salt and coarsely ground black pepper

PARSNIP PUREE
4 parsnips, peeled and cut into 1-inch chunks
2 Tbsp unsalted butter or extra-virgin olive oil
Sea salt and coarsely ground black pepper

LENTILS
2 cups dried Laird, beluga, or Le Puy lentils, picked over, rinsed, and drained
6 cups cold water
2 cloves garlic, crushed
2 bay leaves
2 sprigs thyme
Sea salt and coarsely ground black pepper

ARCTIC CHAR
4 (4 to 5 oz) skin-on arctic char fillets
Sea salt and coarsely ground black pepper
1 Tbsp canola oil
2 Tbsp unsalted butter
1 lemon, halved
¼ cup chopped flat-leaf parsley, for garnish
¼ cup chopped toasted hazelnuts, for garnish

LEMON, CAPER, AND SCALLION MAYO

1 egg
1 egg yolk
1½ tsp Dijon mustard
1½ tsp whole grain mustard
Zest and juice of 1 lemon
1 cup canola oil
1 Tbsp capers, drained
1 Tbsp chopped scallions
Sea salt and coarsely ground black pepper

COLESLAW

2 cups shredded green cabbage
2 cups shredded red cabbage
1 cup chopped kale, stems removed
1 jalapeño, seeded and thinly sliced with a mandoline
¼ cup Lemon Vinaigrette (page 77)

CHIPS

Canola oil, for deep-frying
4 large Yukon gold potatoes such as Kennebec potatoes, peeled or unpeeled
Sea salt, to taste

FISH

3 cups cold water
2 cups Nextjen Gluten-Free Fish & Chip Batter Mix, plus extra for dusting (see Notes)
1½ lb wild Pacific cod, lingcod, or wild salmon, cut into 8 portions
Sea salt, to taste
1 to 2 lemons, cut into wedges

Pacific cod makes for incredible fish and chips, especially when you keep the batter simple enough to let the fish be the star. Nextjen Gluten-Free Fish & Chip Batter Mix is usually my go-to because it's so easy and results in a wonderfully crispy coating. (Plus, it's made by my friends chefs Jennifer Peters and Hamid Salimian.) But no matter the batter, I always serve this dish with homemade lemon-caper mayo, lemony coleslaw, and a handful of freshly cooked fries made with Kennebec potatoes—the best variety for french fries. If you're not up to making your own, salt and vinegar chips make an excellent substitute.

NED'S FISH 'N' CHIPS

MAYO In a food processor or blender, blend together the egg, egg yolk, both mustards, and lemon zest and juice. With the machine running, gradually add the oil in a thin, steady stream, until thick, creamy, and emulsified. Add the capers and scallions. Taste and season with salt and pepper and lemon juice if desired. Can be made ahead of time; will keep refrigerated for up to 3 days.

COLESLAW Combine all the ingredients in a bowl and toss.

CHIPS Heat several inches of oil in a deep heavy-bottomed saucepan, Dutch oven, or deep-fryer to 325°F. Using the fry cutter blade of a mandoline, cut the potatoes into sticks. (Alternatively, use a knife to cut them into ½-inch-thick sticks.) Rinse under cold running water. Pat-dry with paper towels.

Working in batches, gently lower the potatoes into the hot oil, and deep-fry for 2 to 3 minutes, just long enough to cook them but not crisp them (they'll be pale and floppy). Using a slotted spoon, transfer the fries to a plate lined with paper towels. Allow to cool.

Preheat the oven to 200°F. Increase the oil temperature to 375°F. Working in batches, cook the fries again for 3 to 5 minutes or until golden brown and crispy. Using a slotted spoon, transfer to a plate lined with paper towels to drain. In a large bowl, toss the fries with salt. Place in the oven to keep warm while you cook the fish.

FISH In a large bowl, whisk together the water and batter mix. Set aside for 5 minutes.

Allow the temperature of the oil used to fry the potatoes to drop to 350°F. Dust the fish in flour. Working in batches, dip the fish in the batter, letting the excess drip off, and carefully lower into the hot oil. Fry for 5 minutes or until golden brown and crispy. Using a slotted spoon, transfer the fish to a plate lined with paper towels. Season with salt.

Divide the fish and chips among plates, and serve with the coleslaw, mayo dip, and lemon wedges.

CHEF'S NOTES: Create your own gluten-free batter mix: combine 2 cups of your favorite all-purpose gluten-free flour blend (choose one that's heavy on rice and tapioca flours, not garbanzo [chickpea] flour), 1 teaspoon salt, ½ teaspoon pepper, and a few pinches of dry mustard and garlic powder.

For a beer-battered fish, replace the water in the batter with a nonhoppy beer.

One way of respecting and preserving our ocean bounty is to go with smaller portions of high-quality, sustainable fish—even to use seafood as a garnish—and make vegetables the most important thing on the plate. In this dish, I give broccoli the star treatment by preparing it three different ways—raw, roasted, and pureed. This makes for an exciting interplay of textures and flavors. You'll need two bunches of broccoli, or about four heads with stalks, and virtually none of it will go to waste. Shave three stalks into a salad, use two crowns in the puree, and roast the remaining stems and crowns to bring out their natural sweetness.

SERVES 4

BROCCOLI SALAD
3 broccoli stalks
2 Tbsp extra-virgin olive oil
1 Tbsp lemon juice
Sea salt and coarsely
    ground black pepper

BROCCOLI PUREE
2 broccoli crowns,
    separated into florets
1 Tbsp extra-virgin olive oil
Sea salt and coarsely
    ground black pepper

CARAMELIZED BROCCOLI
1 head broccoli, crown and
    stalk separated
2 Tbsp olive oil
Sea salt and coarsely
    ground black pepper

PACIFIC COD WITH BROCCOLI THREE WAYS

BROCCOLI SALAD Trim the ends of the broccoli stalks, and remove the tough outer layer of the stalk. Using a mandoline or vegetable peeler, thinly shave the broccoli lengthwise into ribbons. Place in a bowl and toss with the oil and lemon juice. Season with salt and pepper to taste.

BROCCOLI PUREE Bring a large pot of salted water to a boil over high heat. Set a large bowl of ice water nearby. Add the broccoli to the boiling water and blanch for 30 to 45 seconds or until vibrant green and slightly cooked. Using tongs or a slotted spoon, transfer immediately to the ice water to stop the cooking. Drain and transfer to a blender. Puree for about 30 seconds or until smooth. Add the olive oil and season with salt and pepper.

CARAMELIZED BROCCOLI Trim the bottom of the broccoli stalk and remove the tough outer layer. Slice the stalk into ¼-inch-thick coins. Cut the broccoli crowns into 1-inch florets.

Heat the olive oil in a large skillet set over medium-high heat. Add the broccoli stems and florets, cover, and allow to steam in their own moisture for about 2 minutes or until just tender and beginning to brown. Uncover, stir, and season with salt and pepper to taste. Continue cooking for about 2 minutes or until crispy and golden brown but not overcooked. (You want to create a caramelized flavor but retain the texture of the broccoli.)

COD
1 egg
2 Tbsp milk or water
⅔ cup all-purpose flour
1 tsp garlic powder
½ tsp cayenne pepper
Sea salt and coarsely
   ground black pepper
4 (4 to 5 oz) skinless Pacific
   cod fillets
Vegetable oil, for frying
1 lemon, cut into wedges

COD Whisk the egg and milk (or water) together in a wide, shallow bowl. In a separate wide, shallow bowl, whisk together the flour, garlic powder, and cayenne, and salt and pepper to taste.

Dip a fillet in the egg mixture, letting the excess drip off. Dip in the flour mixture and coat on all sides, shaking off the excess. Repeat with the remaining fillets.

Heat ¼ inch of oil in a heavy-bottomed skillet set over medium-high heat until almost smoking. Add the fillets in an even layer, and fry until golden brown, about 3 minutes. Flip over and fry the other side for another 3 minutes or until golden brown. Transfer to a paper-towel-lined plate. Season with salt and pepper. (If you need to fry the fish in batches, keep the cooked fish warm in a 200°F oven.)

To assemble, spoon the puree onto each plate, then add the shaved broccoli salad and caramelized broccoli. Place the fish on top and serve with lemon wedges.

CITRUS MAYO

2 eggs
2 egg yolks
3 Tbsp Dijon mustard
Zest and juice of 2 limes
Zest and juice of 2 lemons
1 tsp sea salt
1 tsp coarsely ground black pepper
2 cups canola oil

BLUEBERRY RELISH

2 tsp canola oil
1 small shallot, finely chopped
1½ cups fresh or frozen blueberries (divided)
1½ Tbsp honey
1½ Tbsp balsamic vinegar
½ tsp sea salt
½ tsp coarsely ground black pepper

FENNEL SLAW

1 bulb fennel, halved and core removed
1 Tbsp extra-virgin olive oil
1 Tbsp lemon juice (½ lemon)
Sea salt and coarsely ground black pepper

ROASTED HALIBUT

4 (4 to 5 oz) skinless halibut fillets
Sea salt and coarsely ground black pepper
1 Tbsp canola oil
2 Tbsp unsalted butter
2 sprigs thyme, leaves only
1 lemon, halved
4 soft hamburger buns, to serve
4 butter lettuce leaves, to serve
4 dill pickles, halved lengthwise, to serve

SERVES 4

HALIBUT BURGER WITH BLUEBERRY RELISH

CITRUS MAYO In a food processor or blender (or use an immersion blender), combine the eggs, egg yolks, mustard, lime zest and juice, lemon zest and juice, and salt and pepper. With the machine running, slowly add the oil in a thin steady stream until the mixture is emulsified and thickened and all the oil has been incorporated. Taste and adjust seasoning with more salt, pepper, or citrus if desired. Can be made ahead of time; will keep refrigerated for up to 3 days.

BLUEBERRY RELISH Heat the oil in a skillet over medium heat. Add the shallots and sauté for 5 minutes or until tender and translucent. Add 1 cup of the blueberries, honey, vinegar, and salt and pepper. Cook for 12 minutes or until saucy and the blueberries have broken down. Remove the pan from the heat and stir in the remaining ½ cup of blueberries. Set aside to cool. (Relish can be made and refrigerated several days ahead.)

FENNEL SLAW Using a mandoline or sharp knife, slice the fennel paper thin. Toss in a bowl with the oil and lemon juice. Season with salt and pepper to taste.

ROASTED HALIBUT Use paper towels to pat the fish dry, and season with salt and pepper. Heat the oil in a heavy-bottomed, ovenproof skillet over medium-high heat until almost smoking. Carefully lay the fish in the pan. (If necessary, cook the fish in batches to prevent overcrowding, which will keep the fish from caramelizing properly.) Reduce the heat to medium and cook for 2 to 3 minutes; a golden crust will have formed on the flesh. Flip the fillets over and add the butter, the thyme, and a squeeze of lemon over each fish. Cook, basting with the buttery juices, for another 3 to 4 minutes or until browned and almost opaque all the way through. Transfer to a plate.

Assemble the burgers with a lettuce leaf and the fish, fennel slaw, and citrus mayo. Serve with blueberry relish and a dill pickle.

Fresh peas are green, grassy, and sweet—to me they are the taste of spring. Since their season is short, I try to make the most of it by cooking them up every which way. In this dish, they're cooked into a silky puree and sautéed until just tender. Then I use their delicate tendrils for a simple salad. It's a springtime trio that would be delicious with any fish, but since halibut fishing begins right around the same time as pea season, I can't resist bringing these two elements together on one plate.

SERVES 4

HALIBUT WITH SPRING PEAS AND SPINACH PEA PUREE

SPINACH PEA PUREE Heat the oil in a large saucepan over medium heat, add the shallots and salt, and sauté for 3 minutes. Add the peas, spinach, and cream, and cook for 1 minute. Transfer the mixture to a blender, puree until smooth, and strain through a fine-mesh sieve. If necessary, add up to ½ cup warm cream to thin out the puree (I prefer it quite thick and rich).

SAUTÉED PEAS Heat the oil in a skillet over medium heat. Add the shallots and sauté for 3 minutes. Add the peas, season with the salt and pepper, and cook for another minute until the peas are tender.

PEA SHOOTS In a bowl, toss the pea shoots with the oil and lemon juice. Season with salt and pepper to taste.

PAN-SEARED HALIBUT Use paper towels to pat the fish dry, and season with salt and pepper. Heat the oil in a heavy-bottomed, ovenproof skillet over medium-high heat until almost smoking. Carefully lay the fish in the pan. (If necessary, cook the fish in batches to prevent overcrowding, which will keep the fish from caramelizing properly.) Reduce the heat to medium and cook for 2 minutes; a golden crust will have formed on the flesh. Flip the fillets over, and add the butter, the thyme, and a squeeze of lemon over each fish. Cook, basting with the buttery juices, for another 3 to 4 minutes or until browned and almost opaque all the way through. Transfer the fish to a plate.

To assemble, spread the spinach-pea puree on each plate. Add the sautéed peas and place the halibut on top. Garnish with the dressed pea shoots, lemon zest, and sea salt. Serve.

SPINACH PEA PUREE
1 Tbsp extra-virgin olive oil
1 shallot, finely chopped
1 tsp sea salt
3 cups fresh or frozen peas
5 cups spinach leaves
½ cup whipping cream, plus extra for thinning

SAUTÉED PEAS
1 Tbsp canola oil
1 Tbsp chopped shallots
1 cup shelled fresh spring peas (from about 1 lb of pods)
¼ tsp sea salt
¼ tsp coarsely ground black pepper

PEA SHOOTS
4 cups pea shoots
1 Tbsp extra-virgin olive oil
1 Tbsp lemon juice
Sea salt and coarsely ground black pepper

PAN-SEARED HALIBUT
4 (4 to 5 oz) skinless halibut fillets
Sea salt and coarsely ground black pepper
1 Tbsp canola oil
2 Tbsp unsalted butter
2 sprigs thyme, leaves only
1 lemon, halved, with zest reserved for garnish
Sea salt, to sprinkle

Halibut—with its mild flavor and firm flesh—is best served with a vegetable accompaniment that is equally subtle, to build layers of flavor and texture without overpowering the fish. Fennel, with its delicate notes of anise, is a perfect partner. Combined with the vibrant orange vinaigrette, this dish sings all the right notes.

SERVES 4

FENNEL PUREE
1 Tbsp canola oil
1 shallot, finely chopped
1 bulb fennel, stalks removed (but reserve some fronds for garnish), chopped
½ tsp sea salt, plus extra for seasoning
1 cup Vegetable Stock (page 138) or water
Coarsely ground black pepper

ROASTED FENNEL
1 bulb fennel, stalks removed, cut into 8 wedges
1 Tbsp olive oil
Sea salt and coarsely ground black pepper

RAW FENNEL
½ bulb fennel, stalks removed, cored
1 Tbsp extra-virgin olive oil
½ Tbsp lemon juice
Sea salt and coarsely ground black pepper

HALIBUT WITH FENNEL AND ORANGE VINAIGRETTE

FENNEL PUREE Heat the oil in a saucepan over medium heat, add the shallots, and sauté for 5 minutes or until tender and translucent. Add the fennel, salt, and vegetable stock (or water). Bring to a boil over high heat, reduce to a simmer, and cook for 20 minutes or until the fennel is tender. Transfer the mixture to a blender or food processor and blend until smooth. Season with additional salt and pepper to taste.

ROASTED FENNEL Preheat the oven to 425°F. In a large bowl, toss the fennel wedges with olive oil until well coated. Season with salt and pepper. Heat a large heavy-bottomed skillet over medium-high heat until hot. Add the fennel wedges, then transfer to the oven to roast for 15 minutes or until browned. Turn wedges over and roast for another 15 to 20 minutes or until golden brown, caramelized, and tender. (Alternatively, you can roast the fennel on a baking sheet. Preheat the sheet in the oven to help accelerate the browning.)

RAW FENNEL Using a mandoline, thinly shave the fennel crosswise. In a medium bowl, toss shaved fennel with the oil and lemon juice. Season with sea salt and pepper to taste.

4 (4 to 5 oz) skin-on halibut
    fillets
Sea salt and coarsely
    ground black pepper
1 Tbsp canola oil
2 Tbsp unsalted butter
4 sprigs thyme
1 lemon, halved
¼ to ½ cup Orange
    Vinaigrette (page 148),
    to drizzle
2 Tbsp chopped fennel
    fronds, for garnish
1 tsp fennel pollen, for
    garnish (see Notes)

PAN-SEARED HALIBUT Preheat the oven to 400°F. Use paper towels to pat the fish dry, and season with salt and pepper. Heat the oil in a heavy-bottomed, ovenproof skillet over medium-high heat until almost smoking. Carefully lay the fish in the pan skin side down. (If necessary, cook the fish in batches to prevent overcrowding, which will keep the fish from caramelizing properly.) Reduce the heat to medium, and cook for 1 minute or until a golden crust forms on the skin. Flip the fillets over, skin side up, and cook for another 2 to 3 minutes or until browned. Place the pan in the oven, and roast for 3 to 4 minutes or until fish is opaque in the center and flakes easily.

Remove from the oven and add the butter and thyme to the pan. Allow the butter to melt while you squeeze the lemon over the fish. Use a spoon to baste each fillet with the buttery juices for about 1 minute. Transfer the fish to a plate and keep warm.

To assemble the dish, spread the fennel puree on each plate and top with roasted fennel and halibut. Drizzle a tablespoon or two of the orange vinaigrette over each fillet. Top with the shaved fennel, chopped fennel fronds, and a ¼ teaspoon fennel pollen.

CHEF'S NOTES: Fennel pollen is the pollen collected from the flowers of wild fennel. The flavor is reminiscent of fennel but even more complex and floral. There really is no substitute, and though you could skip it, it really does add wonderful dimension to this dish. And once you get a taste, you'll find yourself using it in many other dishes too—pork, chicken, pastas, salads. Look for it at specialty grocery stores or online retailers.

1 lb live clams

4 (4 to 5 oz) skin-on halibut fillets

Sea salt and coarsely ground black pepper

1 Tbsp olive oil, plus extra if needed

¼ cup finely chopped celery hearts

1 shallot, finely chopped

1 clove garlic, thinly sliced

¼ tsp chili flakes

¼ cup white wine

1 Tbsp unsalted butter

1 cup soda water, mineral water, Fish Stock (page 90), or Vegetable Stock (page 138)

2 summer squash, shaved into ribbons with a vegetable peeler

¼ cup chopped celery leaves

2 tsp extra-virgin olive oil whisked with 1 tsp lemon juice

2 Tbsp chopped fresh chives, chervil, or flat-leaf parsley

Artisan bread, to serve

SERVES 4

For this aromatic seafood soup, I use the really tender pale-yellow stalks and leaves from the heart of the celery. They give body and sweetness to the broth and aren't as crunchy and bitter as the outer stalks. I also prefer to use soda or mineral water to really let the light flavors of the ingredients shine through: the water's minerals tenderize the vegetables, preserve their color, and neutralize some of the acidity. This one-pot dish calls for artisan-baked bread, with a nice crust, to mop up every last drop of broth.

BAKED HALIBUT WITH SPICY CLAM BROTH, SUMMER SQUASH, AND CELERY

Rinse the clams under cold running water for at least 5 minutes, and discard any that are open and won't close when tapped or that have broken shells. Scrub off any debris.

Preheat the oven to 400°F. Use paper towels to pat the fish dry, and season with salt and pepper. Heat the oil in a heavy-bottomed, ovenproof skillet over medium-high heat until almost smoking. Add the fish skin side down, and reduce the heat to medium. Cook for about 1 minute or until a golden crust forms on the skin. Transfer to a plate.

Set the skillet back over medium heat and add the celery hearts and shallots (add a little more oil if necessary). Sauté for 3 minutes or until shallots are tender and translucent. Add the garlic and chili flakes and sauté for another minute.

Pour in wine, stirring to scrape up any browned bits, then add the butter and soda water or mineral water (or stock), stirring until the butter is melted. Return fish fillets back to the pan skin side up along with the clams. Cover and transfer the pan to the oven and bake for 5 to 6 minutes or until the fish is almost opaque all the way through and the clams have opened. Discard any clams that have not opened.

Add the squash ribbons, celery leaves, olive oil whisked with lemon juice, and fresh herbs. Cook for about 1 minute, just to heat through. Divide among shallow bowls and serve with slices of artisan bread.

SERVES 4

ROASTED LINGCOD WITH WHITE BEANS, CELERY ROOT, CELERY HEARTS, AND PEAR BUTTER

WHITE BEANS Preheat the oven to 325°F. Pick through the beans and discard any stones, debris, or shriveled beans. Rinse well, transfer to a large pot, and add the water, bay leaf, and onion. Cover and bring to a boil over high heat. Transfer to the oven and cook for 1 hour. Stir in the salt and cook for another 30 minutes or until tender. Drain and set aside. (Can be made and refrigerated several days ahead. Rewarm before serving.)

PEAR BUTTER Combine all the ingredients in a large pot, and bring to a boil over medium heat. Reduce the heat to low and simmer for 1 hour or until the liquid is reduced by half and the fruit is tender. Transfer the mixture to a blender or food processor and blend until smooth. Press the mixture through a fine-mesh sieve to remove the skins. Transfer to an airtight container, and refrigerate until ready to use. (Pear butter will keep for several weeks, or freeze for longer storage. Rewarm before serving.)

CELERY ROOT PUREE In a medium saucepan, combine the celery root with enough cold water to cover. Cover the pot, bring to a boil over high heat, reduce to a simmer, and cook for about 30 minutes or until tender.

Drain, transfer to a blender, and puree until smooth. Season with salt and pepper and stir in the butter or olive oil. (Puree can be made several days ahead and refrigerated. Rewarm before serving.)

CELERY HEARTS Melt the butter in a skillet over medium-high heat. Add the celery hearts, and sauté for about 5 minutes or until golden and crisp-tender. Season with salt and pepper.

LINGCOD Preheat the oven to 400°F, and line a baking sheet with aluminum foil. Season the fish with salt and pepper, place it on the baking sheet, and bake for 7 to 9 minutes or until opaque almost all the way through. Set aside.

To assemble, spread the celery root puree on each plate, add the white beans and celery hearts, and place the fish on top. Spoon some pear butter over the fish and serve.

CHEF'S NOTES: Peel the gnarly outer layer from a celery root with a sharp knife. Cut off the top and bottom of the root to create a stable base, then cut away the outer layer until you get to the creamy white flesh beneath.

WHITE BEANS
1 cup dried white navy beans
3 cups cold water
1 bay leaf
½ onion, quartered
½ tsp sea salt

PEAR BUTTER
1¼ lb ripe pears, unpeeled, cored, and chopped
1 cup pear or fresh apple juice
¼ cup honey or maple syrup
¼ cup white wine vinegar
½ Tbsp salt

CELERY ROOT PUREE
1 large celery root (about 1½ lb), peeled and diced (see Notes)
2 Tbsp sea salt
Coarsely ground black pepper
2 Tbsp unsalted butter or extra-virgin olive oil

CELERY HEARTS
2 Tbsp unsalted butter
1 lb celery hearts, ends trimmed, cut into 2-inch lengths
Sea salt and coarsely ground black pepper
Celery heart leaves, for garnish

LINGCOD
4 (4 to 5 oz) skinless lingcod fillets
Sea salt and coarsely ground black pepper

A feast of umami, this lingcod and mushroom dish is the stuff of winter's-night dinner parties, when there's nowhere you'd rather be than indoors, cozy with your loved ones. Luxury ingredients, such as the black truffle paste in the dressing, are an investment—but a little goes a long way. I prefer truffle paste rather than oil for its subdued aroma and flavor, which allows the other elements to be more assertive. Buy it at gourmet markets or through online retailers.

SERVES 4

LINGCOD WITH MUSHROOMS AND BLACK TRUFFLE VINAIGRETTE

BLACK TRUFFLE VINAIGRETTE Combine the lemon zest and juice, mustard, honey, truffle paste, and salt in a medium bowl. While whisking, slowly drizzle the oil in a thin steady stream until incorporated and the mixture is emulsified. Adjust seasoning to taste. (Alternatively, you can do this in a blender or small food processor.) Can be made ahead of time; will keep refrigerated for up to 2 weeks (although the lemon flavor will start to weaken after a few days).

MUSHROOM PUREE Heat the oil in a medium saucepan over medium heat. Add the shallots and sauté for 3 minutes. Add the mushrooms, salt, and thyme. Pour in the broth. Reduce the heat to low, cover, and cook for 10 minutes or until the mushrooms are tender. Remove the thyme sprig and discard. Transfer the mixture into a blender and puree until smooth. Strain through a fine-mesh sieve.

SAUTÉED MUSHROOMS Heat the oil and 1 tablespoon of the butter in a large skillet over medium-high heat. Add the mushrooms in a single layer, season with salt and pepper to taste, and sauté, stirring occasionally, for about 3 minutes or until golden brown. (Don't crowd the mushrooms or they will steam instead of sear. You may have to sauté in batches.) Transfer to a plate.

Reduce the heat to medium and add the remaining tablespoon of butter. Add the shallots and sauté for 2 minutes. Add the garlic and sauté another minute. Stir in the sautéed mushrooms and the chives. Season with salt and pepper to taste.

PAN-SEARED LINGCOD Preheat the oven to 400°F. Use paper towels to pat the fish dry and season with salt and pepper. Heat the oil in a heavy-bottomed, ovenproof skillet over medium-high heat until almost smoking. Carefully lay the fish in the pan. (If necessary, cook the fish in batches to prevent overcrowding.) Reduce the heat to medium and cook for 1 minute or until a golden crust forms on the skin. Flip the fillets over and cook for another 2 to 3 minutes or until browned. Place the pan in the oven and roast for 4 minutes or until fish is opaque in the center and flakes easily.

Remove from the oven and add the butter and thyme to the pan. Allow the butter to melt while you squeeze the lemon over the fish. Use a spoon to baste each fillet with the buttery juices for about 1 minute. Transfer to a plate.

To assemble, spread the mushroom puree on each plate, add the sautéed mushrooms, and top with the fish. Drizzle over the truffle vinaigrette, and garnish with watercress.

BLACK TRUFFLE VINAIGRETTE
Zest and juice of ½ lemon
1½ tsp Dijon mustard
1 tsp honey
1 tsp black truffle paste
¼ tsp sea salt
½ cup canola oil

MUSHROOM PUREE
1 Tbsp olive oil
1 shallot, finely chopped
1 lb cremini or fresh shiitake mushrooms, stemmed and cut into quarters
½ tsp sea salt
1 sprig thyme
2 cups Vegetable Stock (page 138)

SAUTÉED MUSHROOMS
1 Tbsp olive oil
2 Tbsp unsalted butter (divided)
1 lb fresh wild mushrooms, roughly chopped
Sea salt and coarsely ground black pepper
1 shallot, finely chopped
1 clove garlic, finely chopped
2 Tbsp finely chopped fresh chives

PAN-SEARED LINGCOD
4 (4 to 5 oz) skinless lingcod fillets
Sea salt and coarsely ground black pepper
1 Tbsp canola oil
2 Tbsp unsalted butter
2 sprigs thyme, leaves only
1 lemon, halved
½ bunch watercress, stems removed, for garnish

CARAMELIZED CABBAGE
½ green cabbage, cored and
 thinly sliced
2 Tbsp unsalted butter
Sea salt and coarsely
 ground black pepper

MUSTARD CREAM
1 cup sour cream
1 Tbsp whole grain mustard
Juice of ½ lemon
½ tsp sea salt
½ tsp coarsely ground black
 pepper

PICKLE VINAIGRETTE
¼ cup sweet or dill pickle
 brine, from a jar of
 pickles
1 tsp Dijon mustard
1½ tsp white wine vinegar
¼ tsp sea salt
½ cup canola oil
¼ cup extra-virgin olive oil

LINGCOD
4 (4 to 5 oz) skinless lingcod
 fillets
1 Tbsp canola or olive oil
Sea salt and coarsely
 ground black pepper
½ bunch watercress, stems
 removed

SERVES 4

Cabbage is an ingredient we tend to slice for crunchy slaws or simmer in soup until silky. But sautéing is an underrated technique that everyone should embrace. Just 10 minutes in a hot pan caramelizes the crucifer's natural sugars and teases so much sweetness out of its peppery leaves. This hardy vegetable is fantastic alongside mild lingcod, with piquant mustard cream and pickle vinaigrette to liven things up. Bear in mind, lingcod is a lean and structured fish, so it needs to be cooked through, not just done medium-rare.

GRILLED LINGCOD WITH CARAMELIZED CABBAGE, MUSTARD CREAM, AND PICKLE VINAIGRETTE

CARAMELIZED CABBAGE Bring a pot of salted water to a boil over high heat. Set a large bowl of ice water nearby. Add the cabbage to the boiling water and blanch for 20 seconds. Using a slotted spoon, immediately transfer the cabbage to the ice water to stop the cooking. Drain. (You can skip this step if you're in a hurry, but I love blanching vegetables because it helps to tenderize them and set their color.)

Melt the butter in a large skillet over medium-high heat, add the cabbage, season with salt and pepper, and sauté for 10 minutes or until the cabbage is caramelized and golden brown. Keep warm.

MUSTARD CREAM Combine all the ingredients in a bowl, mix well, and adjust seasoning to taste.

PICKLE VINAIGRETTE Combine the pickle brine, mustard, vinegar, and salt in a blender or small food processor. With the machine running, slowly drizzle the canola oil and olive oil in a thin steady stream until incorporated and the mixture is emulsified. Adjust seasoning to taste. Can be made ahead of time; will keep refrigerated for up to 2 weeks.

LINGCOD Preheat the grill to medium-high or preheat the broiler. Rub the fish with oil and season with salt and pepper.

Set the fish on the oiled cooking grate, and grill for about 3 minutes (or set on a baking sheet with aluminum foil and broil 4 inches from the heat). Turn the fish over and grill (or broil) the other side for another 3 minutes or until cooked through and the flesh flakes easily. Remove from the grill and tent with foil to keep warm.

Divide the warm cabbage between 4 plates, and top with the lingcod. Spoon the mustard cream over the fish. Divide the watercress between the plates and drizzle some pickle vinaigrette over all.

SERVES 4

ROCKFISH WITH HONEY AND ROASTED BLACK-PEPPER PLUMS

SPINACH AND WATERCRESS SALAD Toss the spinach, watercress, and almonds in a large bowl. When ready to serve (after the fish is done), toss with just enough vinaigrette to coat. Season with salt and pepper to taste.

PLUMS AND ROCKFISH Preheat the oven to 400°F. Season the plums with salt and a generous amount of black pepper. Heat 1 tablespoon of the butter in a heavy-bottomed, ovenproof skillet over medium-high heat. Once butter stops foaming, add plums and toss to coat in butter. Transfer skillet to oven and roast plums for 2 to 3 minutes or until softened. Return skillet to the stovetop and place over medium heat. Add honey and cook plums another 1 to 2 minutes, basting with the pan juices.

Use paper towels to pat the fish dry, and season with salt and pepper. Heat the oil in another heavy-bottomed, ovenproof skillet over medium-high heat until almost smoking. Carefully lay the fish in the pan skin side down. (If necessary, cook the fish in batches to prevent overcrowding, which will keep the fish from caramelizing properly.) Reduce the heat to medium, cook for 1 minute or until a golden crust forms on the skin, then transfer the skillet to the oven. Roast for 3 minutes. Remove from the oven and flip the fillets over. Add the remaining 1 tablespoon of butter to the skillet. Cook over medium heat, basting with the buttery juices, for another 1 minute or until fish is browned and flakes easily.

Divide the fish and plums between 4 plates, and drizzle with some of the juices from the skillet the plums were cooked in. Divide the salad among the plates and serve.

SPINACH AND WATERCRESS SALAD
1 (5 to 6 oz) bag baby spinach
1 bunch watercress, stems removed
⅓ cup toasted slivered almonds
About ¼ cup Lemon Vinaigrette (page 77)
Sea salt and coarsely ground black pepper

PLUMS AND ROCKFISH
4 plums, quartered
Sea salt and coarsely ground black pepper
2 Tbsp unsalted butter (divided)
2 Tbsp honey
4 (4 to 5 oz) skin-on rockfish fillets
1 Tbsp canola oil

ROCKFISH

1 (3 lb) fresh whole rockfish, scaled and cleaned

2 Tbsp canola oil

Sea salt and coarsely ground black pepper

1 lemon, sliced

3 scallions, trimmed

About ¼ cup Lemon Vinaigrette (page 77), to serve

GRILLED BROCCOLINI OR ASPARAGUS

1 bunch broccolini or 1 lb asparagus, ends trimmed

2 Tbsp olive oil

Sea salt and coarsely ground black pepper

SERVES 2 TO 4

GRILLED WHOLE ROCKFISH WITH LEMON VINAIGRETTE

ROCKFISH Preheat a grill to medium-high or preheat the broiler. Rub the fish with the oil, and season inside and out with salt and pepper. Place the lemon slices and scallions inside the cavity. Score the skin 2 or 3 times on each side to aid in the cooking and to make sure the fish doesn't curl up on the grill.

Set the fish on the oiled cooking grate and grill for about 10 minutes (or set on a baking sheet with aluminum foil and broil 4 inches from the heat). Turn the fish over and grill (or broil) for another 10 minutes or until the skin is lightly charred and crispy and the flesh flakes easily. Remove from the grill and tent with foil to keep warm.

GRILLED BROCCOLINI OR ASPARAGUS Preheat the grill to medium-high or preheat the oven to 400°F. In a large bowl, toss the broccolini or asparagus with the olive oil and salt and pepper to taste until evenly coated. Place on the cooking grate perpendicular to the slats and grill (or place on a baking sheet and bake), turning occasionally, for 7 minutes or until tender and slightly charred (longer if the asparagus is particularly thick). Transfer to a platter.

Serve the fish with grilled broccolini or asparagus, all drizzled with lemon vinaigrette.

CHILI LIME MAYO
1 egg
1 egg yolk
Zest and juice of 1 lime
½ tsp sea salt
½ tsp coarsely ground black pepper
1 cup canola oil
1 to 2 Tbsp Sriracha

QUICKLES
½ cup white wine vinegar
½ cup water
2 Tbsp granulated sugar
1 Tbsp sea salt
¼ tsp chili flakes
½ English cucumber
½ bulb fennel, stalks removed, cored
½ shallot, peeled
½ small carrot

ROCKFISH
4 (4 to 5 oz) skin-on rockfish fillets
Sea salt and coarsely ground black pepper
1 Tbsp canola oil
1 Tbsp unsalted butter
½ lime
½ cup Chili Lime Mayo (see above), to serve
8 slices seedy bread or herbed focaccia, toasted or grilled, to serve
4 butter lettuce leaves, to serve

SERVES 4

ROCKFISH SANDWICHES WITH CHILI LIME MAYO AND QUICKLES

CHILI LIME MAYO In a food processor or blender (or use an immersion blender), combine the egg, egg yolk, lime zest and juice, and salt and pepper. With the machine running, slowly add the oil in a thin steady stream. When the mixture is emulsified and thickened and all the oil has been incorporated, add the Sriracha to taste. Taste and adjust seasoning with more salt, pepper, or lime if desired. Can be made ahead of time; will keep refrigerated for up to 3 days.

QUICKLES Combine the vinegar, water, sugar, salt, and chili flakes in a saucepan. Bring to a boil over medium-high heat, and stir until the sugar has dissolved. Set aside to cool completely.

Using a mandoline, slice the cucumber, fennel, shallot, and carrot very thin (about ⅛ inch thick), and transfer to a nonreactive bowl. Pour the cooled pickling liquid over the vegetables, and refrigerate for 2 to 3 hours. (You still want the veggies to retain some texture, so don't let them pickle overnight.)

ROCKFISH Use paper towels to pat the fish dry, and season with salt and pepper. Heat the oil in a heavy-bottomed, ovenproof skillet over medium-high heat until almost smoking. Carefully lay the fish in the pan skin side down. (If necessary, cook the fish in batches to prevent overcrowding, which will keep the fish from caramelizing properly.) Reduce the heat to medium and cook for about 2 minutes; a golden crust will have formed on the skin. Flip the fish, add the butter to the pan, and squeeze the lime over the fish. Cook, basting with the buttery juices, for another 2 to 3 minutes or until browned and the fish is almost opaque all the way through.

To build the sandwiches, spread the mayo on the toasted bread, and add a piece of lettuce, the rockfish, then the quickles. Top with the other slice of bread and serve.

An ancient variety of wheat, farro comes either as a whole grain or semipearled. Its versatility makes it a go-to grain in my book. The nuttiness of this hearty grain goes particularly well with the soy-sesame vinaigrette in this recipe.

SERVES 4

SKATE WITH FARRO, SPROUTED BEANS, AND SOY SESAME VINAIGRETTE

SOY SESAME VINAIGRETTE Combine the lemon zest and juice, soy sauce, mustard, and honey in a small bowl. While whisking, slowly drizzle the canola oil and sesame oil in a thin steady stream until incorporated and the mixture is emulsified. (Alternatively, you can do this with an immersion blender or in a blender or small food processor.) Can be made ahead of time; will keep refrigerated for up to 2 weeks (although the lemon flavor will start to weaken after a few days).

FARRO In a medium saucepan, combine the farro, salt, and enough cold water to cover it by 3 inches. Bring to a boil over medium heat. Cover and cook for 30 minutes or until tender and al dente. Drain the farro.

ROASTED EGGPLANT Preheat the oven to 425°F. Toss the eggplant pieces with both oils on a baking sheet until well coated. Season with salt and pepper. Roast for 20 minutes or until golden brown and tender but not overcooked.

SKATE Use paper towels to pat the fish dry, and season with salt and pepper. Heat the oil in a heavy-bottomed, ovenproof skillet over medium-high heat until almost smoking. Carefully lay the fish in the pan. (If necessary, cook the fish in batches to prevent overcrowding, which will keep the fish from caramelizing properly.) Reduce the heat to medium and cook for 2 minutes; a golden crust will have formed on the flesh. Flip the fillets over and add the butter to the pan. Allow it to melt while you squeeze the lemon over the fish. Use a spoon to baste each fillet with the buttery juices for another 2 to 3 minutes or until fish is cooked through. Transfer to a plate.

To serve, divide the warm farro among serving bowls, add the roasted eggplant, and top with a portion of the skate. Drizzle over the vinaigrette, and garnish with the sprouts, scallions, and sesame seeds.

CHEF'S NOTES: Sprouted beans are incredibly nutritious, and they're delicious sprinkled on this dish. You can find packages of fresh sprouted beans and legumes, such as lentils and garbanzos, at health-focused grocery stores such as Whole Foods. I like the Eatmore Sprouts sprouted bean mix (eatmoresprouts.com).

SOY SESAME VINAIGRETTE
Zest and juice of 1 lemon
2 tsp soy sauce
2 tsp Dijon mustard
1½ tsp honey
½ cup canola oil
1 Tbsp sesame oil

FARRO
1 cup farro, rinsed in cold water and soaked overnight
½ Tbsp sea salt

ROASTED EGGPLANT
1 long Japanese eggplant, cut into 1-inch pieces
1 Tbsp canola oil
½ tsp sesame oil
Sea salt and coarsely ground black pepper

SKATE
1½ lb skate wings
Sea salt and coarsely ground black pepper
1 Tbsp canola oil
1 Tbsp unsalted butter
1 lemon, halved
½ cup sprouted beans, for garnish (see Notes)
1 scallion, chopped, for garnish
Toasted sesame seeds, for garnish

Skate has such a unique ribbed texture that dining on this fish becomes a wonderfully tactile experience. The Asian-inspired preparation here is exciting flavor-wise too: the mushrooms soak up the consommé-like broth, and the sweet-and-spicy cashews complete the dish with their buttery richness and gentle crunch.

SERVES 4

SKATE WITH SHIITAKE MUSHROOM BROTH AND SWEET AND SPICY CASHEWS

SHIITAKE MUSHROOM BROTH Roughly chop all the mushroom stems and half of the caps. (Set aside the remaining half.) Heat the oil in a large pot over medium heat. Add the onions and chopped mushrooms, and sauté for 10 to 15 minutes or until caramelized and deep golden brown. Add the ginger, garlic, and scallions, and sauté for another minute. Pour in the sake, stirring to scrape up the browned bits. Add the water and bring to a boil. Lower the heat and simmer for 20 to 25 minutes or until the broth is reduced by half.

Strain the broth into another pot and season with salt (or soy sauce) to taste. Add another splash of sake and a squeeze of lime.

SWEET AND SPICY CASHEWS Preheat the oven to 375°F. Line a baking sheet with parchment paper. Spread the cashews on the baking sheet and roast for 10 to 12 minutes or until golden brown. Transfer to a medium bowl and toss with the salt, brown sugar, and chili paste until evenly coated. Spread cashews on the baking sheet and return to the oven. Turn the temperature off and let the cashews dry in the oven as it cools down. When cool, roughly chop.

SKATE Use paper towels to pat the fish dry, and season with salt and pepper. Heat 1 tablespoon of the oil in a heavy-bottomed, ovenproof sauté pan over medium-high heat until almost smoking. Carefully lay the fish in the pan. (If necessary, cook the fish in batches to prevent overcrowding, which will keep the fish from caramelizing properly.) Reduce the heat to medium and cook for 2 minutes; a golden crust will have formed on the flesh. Flip the fillets over and add the butter to the pan. Allow it to melt while you squeeze the lemon over the fish. Use a spoon to baste each fillet with the buttery juices for another 2 to 3 minutes or until fish is cooked through. Transfer to a plate.

Slice the remaining shiitake caps. Heat the remaining tablespoon of oil in the pan over medium-high heat, and add the sliced mushrooms. Sauté until moisture cooks off and mushrooms are caramelized, about 5 minutes. Add the Chinese broccoli, snow peas, and sugar snap peas, and sauté until crisp-tender, about 1 minute. Add the broth and bring to a simmer over medium-high heat.

Divide the vegetables and broth among shallow bowls, place the fish on top, and garnish with the raw enoki mushrooms and sweet-and-spicy cashews.

SHIITAKE MUSHROOM BROTH
1 lb fresh shiitake mushrooms, stems and caps separated
3 Tbsp canola oil
1 onion, finely chopped
3 Tbsp peeled, chopped fresh ginger
6 cloves garlic, crushed
2 scallions
2 cups sake, plus extra for finishing
4 cups water
Sea salt or soy sauce
½ lime

SWEET AND SPICY CASHEWS
1½ cups cashews
½ tsp sea salt
2 tsp brown sugar
1 Tbsp chili paste such as Sriracha or sambal oelek

SKATE
1½ lb skate wings
Sea salt and coarsely ground black pepper
2 Tbsp canola oil (divided)
1 Tbsp unsalted butter
½ lemon
3 stalks Chinese broccoli (gai lan), sliced lengthwise
½ cup sliced snow peas
½ cup sliced sugar snap peas
Enoki mushrooms, for garnish

SERVES 4

4 (4 to 5 oz) skinless sturgeon fillets
Sea salt and coarsely ground black pepper
¼ cup olive oil
1½ cups cherry tomatoes
½ cup sun-dried tomatoes, chopped (drain if packed in oil)
1 (15 oz) can chickpeas, drained
20 green olives (about 1 cup), pitted (optional)
2 cloves garlic, chopped
2 Tbsp capers, drained
2 Tbsp chopped flat-leaf parsley
2 Tbsp extra-virgin olive oil
1 Tbsp lemon juice
Warm crusty bread, to serve

ROASTED STURGEON WITH TOMATO CONFIT, CAPERS, CHICKPEAS, AND PARSLEY

Preheat the oven to 400°F. Use paper towels to pat the fish dry, and season with salt and pepper. Heat the oil in a heavy-bottomed, ovenproof skillet over medium-high heat until almost smoking. Carefully lay the fish in the pan. (If necessary, cook the fish in batches to prevent overcrowding, which will keep the fish from caramelizing properly.) Reduce the heat to medium and cook for 1 minute or until a golden crust forms on the flesh. Set in the oven and roast for 5 minutes.

Flip the fillets over and add the cherry tomatoes, sun-dried tomatoes, chickpeas, olives, and garlic. Return to the oven and roast another 5 minutes.

Remove from the oven and baste the fillets with the pan juices. Add the capers, parsley, olive oil, and lemon juice. Taste and adjust seasoning with more salt and pepper if desired.

Divide among 4 plates and serve with warm crusty bread for sopping up the juices.

Citrus butter–roasted sturgeon makes a mouth-watering foundation for bold and contrasting complements. The grassy watercress pesto nods to summer, while the lentils, walnuts, and maple syrup capture the taste of fall.

MAPLE VINAIGRETTE
¼ cup red wine or sherry
    vinegar
1 Tbsp Dijon mustard
¼ cup maple syrup
½ tsp sea salt
½ cup canola oil
¼ cup extra-virgin olive oil

LENTILS
1 cup dried Laird, beluga,
    or Le Puy lentils, picked
    over, rinsed, and drained
3 cups cold water
¼ onion
1 bay leaf
1 sprig thyme
Sea salt and coarsely
    ground black pepper

CANDIED WALNUTS
1 cup walnuts or almonds
1 Tbsp maple syrup
Sea salt and coarsely
    ground black pepper

**WATERCRESS AND
WALNUT PESTO**
½ lb watercress, stems
    removed, plus a few
    leaves reserved for
    garnish
½ lb spinach, stems
    trimmed
¼ cup toasted walnuts or
    slivered almonds
¼ cup extra-virgin olive oil
Zest and juice of ½ lemon
½ tsp sea salt
½ tsp coarsely ground black
    pepper

STURGEON
¼ cup (½ stick) unsalted
    butter, softened
Zest of 1 lemon
4 (4 to 5 oz) skinless
    sturgeon fillets
Sea salt and coarsely
    ground black pepper

BAKED STURGEON WITH LENTILS, WATERCRESS PESTO, AND MAPLE VINAIGRETTE

MAPLE VINAIGRETTE Combine the vinegar, mustard, maple syrup, and salt in a small bowl. While whisking, slowly drizzle the canola oil and olive oil in a thin steady stream until incorporated and the mixture is emulsified. Adjust seasoning to taste. (Alternatively, you can do this with an immersion blender or in a blender or small food processor.) Can be made ahead of time; will keep refrigerated for up to 2 weeks.

LENTILS In a large saucepan, combine the lentils, water, onion, bay leaf, and thyme. Bring to a boil over high heat, reduce to low, cover, and simmer for 25 minutes or until tender. Drain off any excess water. Remove and discard the onion, bay leaf, and thyme. Season lentils with salt and pepper to taste. (Can be made several days ahead and refrigerated. Reheat before serving.)

CANDIED WALNUTS Preheat the oven to 325°F. In a medium bowl, toss the walnuts (or almonds) with the maple syrup until evenly coated. Sprinkle with salt and pepper. Transfer to a parchment-lined baking sheet. Bake for 25 minutes, stirring halfway through cooking time, or until they smell toasted and are lightly browned. The nuts will crisp up as they cool. (Can be made several weeks ahead and stored in an airtight container.)

WATERCRESS AND WALNUT PESTO Bring a large pot of salted water to a boil over high heat. Set a large bowl of ice water nearby. Add the watercress and spinach to the boiling water, and blanch for 30 seconds. Use tongs or a slotted spoon to transfer immediately to the ice water. When completely cool, drain.

Squeeze the greens over a colander in the sink to extract as much water as possible. Transfer the greens to a blender or food processor, add the walnuts (or almonds), olive oil, lemon zest and juice, and salt and pepper. Puree until smooth and creamy. (Can be made several days ahead and refrigerated.)

STURGEON Preheat the oven to 400°F. In a small bowl, mix together the butter and lemon zest.

Use paper towels to pat the fish dry, and season both sides with salt and pepper. Set on a baking sheet lined with aluminum foil. Top each fillet with a tablespoon of the citrus butter. Bake for 12 to 15 minutes or until the flesh is cooked through and flakes easily.

To serve, divide the lentils among the plates and top with a sturgeon fillet. Spoon pesto over the fish and drizzle maple vinaigrette over all. Garnish with candied walnuts and fresh watercress leaves.

SERVES 4

STURGEON WITH SAVORY KELP CREAM

KELP CREAM Heat the oil in a large saucepan over medium heat, add the shallots and garlic, and sauté for 30 seconds or until fragrant. Add the remaining ingredients, except the salt, bring to a simmer over medium heat, and cook for 5 minutes. Remove the pan from the heat and cool lightly.

Transfer the mixture to a blender or food processor and process until smooth. Strain the puree through a fine-mesh sieve. Thin out, if desired, with a little extra cream. Season to taste with salt. (Can be made ahead and refrigerated. Warm gently over low heat before serving.)

STURGEON Preheat the oven to 400°F. Use paper towels to pat the fish dry, and season both sides with salt and pepper. Heat the oil in a heavy-bottomed, ovenproof skillet over medium-high heat until almost smoking. Carefully lay the fish in the pan. (If necessary, cook the fish in batches to prevent overcrowding, which will keep the fish from caramelizing properly.) Reduce the heat to medium and cook for 1 minute or until a golden crust forms on the flesh. Set in the oven and roast for 5 minutes.

Flip the fillets over, return to the oven, and roast another 5 minutes or until flesh flakes easily.

To serve, divide the sturgeon among the plates and spoon some of the kelp cream over the top. Garnish with nori and sesame seeds.

KELP CREAM
½ Tbsp canola oil
½ shallot, finely chopped
1 small clove garlic, finely chopped
1 Thai bird chile, seeded and finely chopped
1½ cups whipping cream, plus extra if needed
1 cup kelp, rinsed (if dried, soak in warm water for 10 minutes)
Zest of ½ lime
½ tsp sesame oil
Sea salt, to taste

STURGEON
4 (4 to 5 oz) skinless sturgeon fillets
Sea salt and coarsely ground black pepper
1 Tbsp canola oil
Dried nori, sliced into thin strips, for garnish
Toasted sesame seeds, for garnish

FATTY FISH

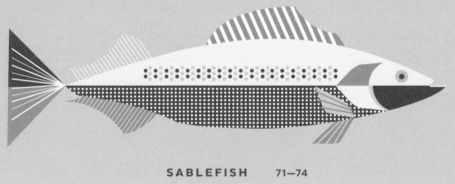

SABLEFISH   71—74

[profile 203]

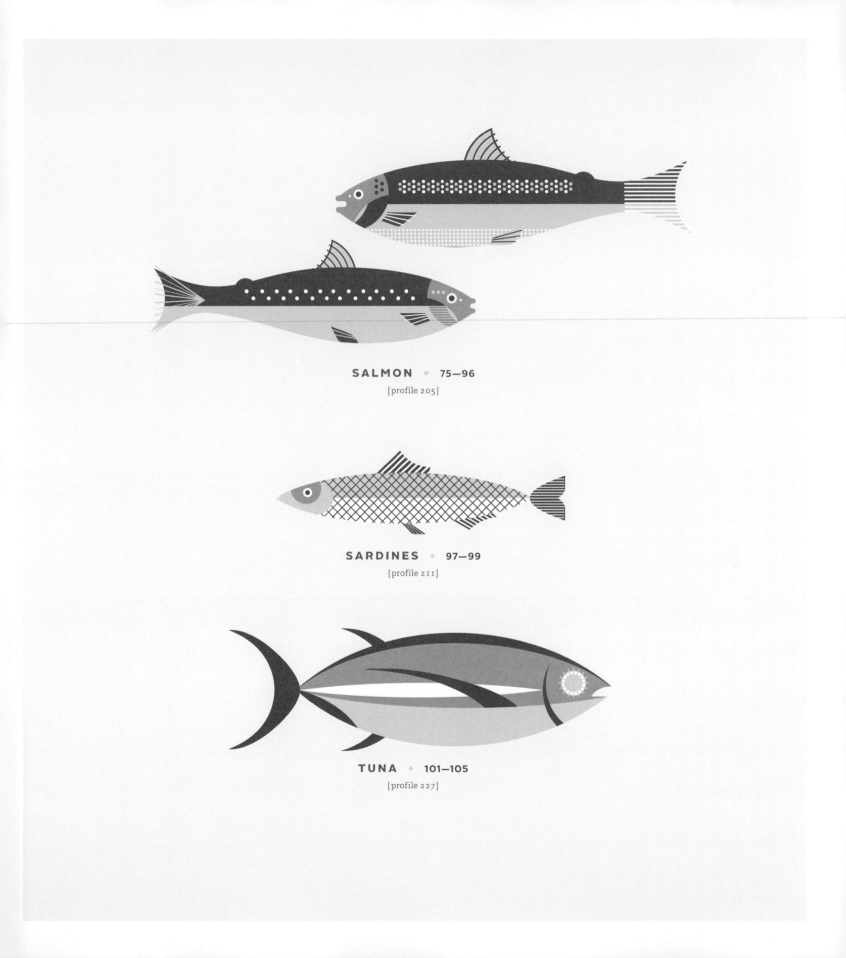

SALMON • 75—96

[profile 205]

SARDINES • 97—99

[profile 211]

TUNA • 101—105

[profile 227]

FATTY FISH

WE CAN BE a little fat-phobic in North America, but that needs to change. Our bodies need natural fats to be healthy, and the fish in this section are rich in the healthiest fats of all—omega-3 fatty acids. These nutritional powerhouses lower the risk of heart disease and are essential to brain function.

Wild salmon is a gift to West Coasters, as the First Nations have recognized for millennia. The original inhabitants of the West Coast celebrate the role of this iconic fish in the cycle of life—alongside the whales, bears, eagles, and trees—in their oral history and works of art.

When it comes to our oil-rich fishy friends, favor dry-heat cooking methods: baking, grilling, and roasting. To keep fatty fish dishes from becoming too heavy, be stingy with the cooking oil or butter, and save your creamy sauces for leaner white species. The shimmering blue and gray fatty species love a stint in the smoker for extra layers of rich flavor, and they take on subtle forest flavors when planked.

Oil-rich fish need complements that will cut through their fattiness, so ramp up the acidity with ingredients such as lemons, tomatoes, apples, and cranberries. Salmon and capers are a no-brainer, but have you thought of this fish with pickled cherries or chiles for next-level contrast? Oily fish also pair well with vegetables such as green beans, Brussels sprouts, and summer squash, whose mild bitterness balances the richness of the natural fats.

I encourage you to try my Smoked Sablefish and Apple Chowder (page 71) to get a sense of how amazing oily fish can be in a well-balanced dish. Creamy and comforting, this soup wins over adults and kids alike. Planked Wild Salmon with Nectarines (page 85) is the ultimate taste of summer: it's uncomplicated yet packed with flavor. And if you've been searching for the Best Tuna Melt Ever, you're in luck because it's right here on page 104. The secret ingredients—artichoke hearts and sharp aged cheddar—make this the most flavor-packed version you'll ever sink your teeth into.

Ocean Wise throws an annual Chowder Chowdown in cities across Canada. It's a friendly competition that challenges chefs to come up with interesting recipes based on local, sustainable ingredients. This creamy yet light chowder of mine won the trophy in 2014 at the Vancouver edition. The smoked sablefish has the mouthwatering flavor and aroma of freshly sizzled bacon, so pairing it with tart-sweet Granny Smiths was a no-brainer. I layer the apple component into the dish in both the velvety broth and as a crisp raw apple garnish. You could certainly buy premade apple butter, but if you have the time to make it from scratch, it's well worth it.

SERVES 4 TO 6

SMOKED SABLEFISH AND APPLE CHOWDER

APPLE BUTTER Combine all the ingredients in a large pot, and bring to a boil. Reduce the heat to low and simmer for 1 hour or until the liquid is reduced by half and the fruit is tender. Transfer the mixture to a blender or food processor and blend until smooth. Press the mixture through a fine-mesh sieve to remove the skins. Transfer to an airtight container and refrigerate. (This recipe makes extra. Apple butter will keep for several weeks, or freeze for longer storage. Gently warm before serving on the fish.)

CHOWDER Heat the oil in a large pot over medium heat. Add the onions, celery, and fennel, and sauté for 7 minutes or until vegetables are softened and translucent. Add the garlic, season with a pinch of salt and pepper, and cook about 1 minute more or until fragrant. Add the potatoes and thyme and bay leaves, then pour in the wine (or beer), stirring to scrape up the browned bits.

Stir in the milk and cream. Bring to a simmer over medium-high heat, reduce to medium-low, and cook for 15 minutes. Add the sablefish and corn, and cook for another 5 minutes or until the potatoes are tender and fish is warmed through. Taste and adjust seasoning with more salt and pepper if desired.

Ladle the soup into individual bowls, add a tablespoon or two of shredded apple, and sprinkle with the chives (or scallions). Dot each bowl with a teaspoon or two of the apple butter, and drizzle with olive oil.

CHEF'S NOTES: Try using fruit butters with roasted halibut, spot prawns, scallops, and even salmon ice cream! Create variations by replacing the apples with quince or stone fruits such as peaches, apricots, and nectarines.

APPLE BUTTER
1½ lb tart apples such as Granny Smith, unpeeled, cored, and chopped
1 cup apple juice
¼ cup honey or maple syrup
2 Tbsp white wine vinegar
1½ tsp sea salt

CHOWDER
2 Tbsp olive oil
½ onion, diced
1 stalk celery, diced
½ bulb fennel, cored and diced
2 cloves garlic, chopped
Sea salt and coarsely ground black pepper
2 large Yukon gold potatoes, peeled and cut into ½-inch cubes
2 sprigs thyme
2 bay leaves
1 cup white wine or pale ale (not too hoppy)
4 cups whole milk
2 cups whipping cream
1 lb golden smoked sablefish, skinned, deboned, and diced
1 cup fresh or frozen corn kernels
1 Granny Smith apple, unpeeled and shredded
¼ cup chopped fresh chives or scallions
Apple Butter (see above)
Extra-virgin olive oil, for drizzling

Here sablefish is seared until the skin is crispy and caramelized, and then served with a sprinkle of crunchy, buttery cashews. A trio of cauliflower preparations—roasted, pureed, and shaved raw—echoes these textures and flavors, while a swipe of tart cranberry chutney brings it all to life.

SERVES 4

SABLEFISH WITH CRANBERRIES, CASHEWS, AND CAULIFLOWER

CRANBERRY CHUTNEY Combine all the ingredients in a medium saucepan over medium-low heat, and cook for 30 minutes or until the cranberries are tender and the mixture is thickened and saucy. Taste and adjust seasonings with up to 1 teaspoon salt or 1 tablespoon red wine vinegar, if needed. The sweet, salty, and sour flavors should be balanced. Transfer the cranberry sauce to a blender or food processor, and blend until slightly chunky. (Chutney can be made several days ahead and refrigerated. Allow to come to room temperature before serving.)

CAULIFLOWER THREE WAYS For the puree, steam half the cauliflower (about 5 cups) in a steamer insert set over a few inches of boiling water for 12 minutes or until tender but not overcooked. Transfer the cauliflower to a blender, add 2 tablespoons of the olive oil (or butter) and 1 teaspoon salt, and puree until smooth.

For the roasted cauliflower, preheat the oven to 400°F. In a large bowl, toss 3 cups of the remaining florets with 1 tablespoon of the olive oil. Season with salt and pepper and toss to coat. Arrange in a single layer on a rimmed baking sheet. Roast in the oven for 10 to 15 minutes or until florets are evenly caramelized and golden brown. Toss with 1 tablespoon butter if desired.

For the raw cauliflower, use a mandoline to shave the remaining florets (about 2 cups) lengthwise as thinly as possible. Transfer to a medium bowl and toss with the remaining 2 teaspoons olive oil, the lemon juice, and salt to taste.

SABLEFISH Preheat the oven to 400°F. Use paper towels to pat the fish dry, and season with salt and pepper. Heat the oil in a heavy-bottomed, ovenproof skillet over medium-high heat until almost smoking. Carefully lay the fish in the pan skin side down. (If necessary, cook the fish in batches to prevent overcrowding.) Reduce the heat to medium, and cook for 1 minute or until a golden crust forms on the skin. Flip the fillets over and cook for another 2 to 3 minutes or until browned. Place the pan in the oven and roast for 4 minutes or until fish is opaque in the center and flakes easily.

Remove from the oven and add the butter to the pan. Allow it to melt while you squeeze the lemon over the fish. Baste each fillet with the buttery juices for about 1 minute. Transfer the fish to a plate and keep warm.

Spread the cauliflower puree on each plate. Add the fillets and surround with roasted cauliflower. Spoon 2 tablespoons of chutney over the fish, and top with the shaved cauliflower. Garnish with cashews and smoked salt.

CRANBERRY CHUTNEY
3 cups fresh or frozen cranberries (12 oz bag)
½ cup dried cranberries
2 cups cranberry juice (sweet)
¼ cup honey
¼ cup red wine vinegar, plus extra to taste
1½ tsp sea salt, plus extra to taste

CAULIFLOWER THREE WAYS
2 heads cauliflower, florets only (about 10 cups, divided)
3 Tbsp plus 2 tsp olive oil or unsalted butter
Sea salt and coarsely ground black pepper
1 Tbsp butter (optional)
2 tsp lemon juice

SABLEFISH
4 (4 to 5 oz) skin-on sablefish fillets
Sea salt and coarsely ground black pepper
1 Tbsp canola oil
2 Tbsp unsalted butter, softened
1 lemon, halved
Chopped toasted cashews, for garnish
Smoked sea salt, to sprinkle (see Notes on page 146)

Brandade is a classic Mediterranean dish made with salt cod and potatoes, but my version calls for the first Pacific fish I fell in love with: sablefish. I use lightly cured and cold-smoked sablefish because it has more flavor and a firmer structure than fresh, which helps it stand out against the potatoes. If you have a smoker, you can smoke it yourself, or you can order smoked sablefish from gourmet delis or online retailers—just be sure it's naturally golden hued, with no added coloring.

SERVES 4

HORSERADISH VINAIGRETTE
Zest and juice of ½ lemon
1½ tsp Dijon mustard
1 tsp prepared horseradish
¼ tsp sea salt
¼ tsp coarsely ground
    black pepper
½ cup canola oil

SABLEFISH BRANDADE
1 lb Yukon gold potatoes,
    peeled and quartered
1 cup whole milk
½ lb cold-smoked sablefish
    fillets
2 Tbsp unsalted butter
Sea salt and coarsely
    ground black pepper
1 Tbsp whole grain mustard
2 Tbsp chopped fresh
    chives or flat-leaf parsley
Crostini, to serve

SABLEFISH BRANDADE WITH HORSERADISH VINAIGRETTE

HORSERADISH VINAIGRETTE Combine the lemon zest and juice, mustard, horseradish, salt, and pepper in a small bowl. While whisking, slowly drizzle the oil in a thin steady stream until incorporated and the mixture is emulsified. Adjust seasoning to taste. (Alternatively, you can do this with an immersion blender or in a blender or small food processor.) Can be made ahead of time; will keep refrigerated for up to 2 weeks (although the lemon flavor will start to weaken after a few days).

SABLEFISH BRANDADE In a large saucepan, combine the potatoes with enough cold water to cover by 1 inch. Salt generously and bring to a boil over high heat. Cook for 15 to 20 minutes or until tender.

Meanwhile, bring the milk to a simmer in a medium saucepan set over medium-low heat. Add the sablefish, and gently poach for 5 minutes or until the fish is warmed through. Remove the sablefish from the milk, and reserve the milk.

Drain the potatoes and pass them through a ricer or food mill. Alternatively, return them to the pot and mash with a potato masher. Add the butter and stir, mash, or beat with an electric mixer until melted and incorporated. Stir or beat in ½ cup of the reserved milk from poaching the fish, or more if necessary to achieve a silky puree. Season generously with salt and pepper.

Add the fish to the potatoes, along with the mustard and chives (or parsley). Stir well to combine. (You want the fish to break up throughout the potatoes.) Transfer to a serving plate. Drizzle with horseradish vinaigrette and serve with crostini on the side.

Rather than play short-order chef at a family gathering, accommodate all tastes and dietary needs with a build-your-own taco bar. Pink salmon (also called humpback salmon) is a great choice for taco parties because it's economical and its mild flavor is truly enhanced when you add all the delicious garnishes. I prefer the rustic quality of soft corn tortillas over flour tortillas. To make the tacos more structured and decadent, I warm the tortillas up with a couple tablespoons of mozzarella sandwiched between them. All of the components in this recipe scale up nicely, making it easy to prepare these tacos for a crowd.

SERVES 4

SALMON TACOS WITH JALAPEÑO VINAIGRETTE, BLACK BEANS, AND AVOCADO SMASH

BLACK BEANS Preheat the oven to 325°F. Pick through the beans and discard any stones, debris, or shriveled beans. Rinse well, transfer to a large pot, and add the water, bay leaf, and onion. Cover and bring to a boil over high heat. Transfer to the oven and cook for 1 hour. Stir in the salt and continue cooking for another 30 minutes or until tender. Drain and set aside. (Can be made and refrigerated several days ahead. Rewarm before serving.)

JALAPEÑO VINAIGRETTE Preheat the broiler and set the oven rack 4 inches below it. Remove the stem from the jalapeño. Set on a baking sheet and broil for about 5 minutes or until blackened. Turn and roast the other side for 5 minutes or until blackened. Allow to cool, then peel off the skins, and split open and remove the seeds. Chop.

Combine the jalapeño, lime zest and juice, mustard, vinegar, and salt in a blender or small food processor. With the machine running, slowly drizzle the canola oil in a thin steady stream until incorporated and the mixture is emulsified. Adjust seasoning to taste. Set aside. Can be made ahead of time; will keep refrigerated for up to 2 weeks.

TACO SHELLS Preheat a griddle or large skillet over medium heat. Lay a tortilla in the pan, spread 2 tablespoons of mozzarella on the surface, and top with another tortilla. Allow to heat for 30 seconds, turn over and heat for another 20 seconds, or until warmed and the cheese has melted (do not toast until brown and hard). Repeat with the remaining tortillas. Wrap in aluminum foil to keep warm.

SALMON TACOS Preheat the oven to 400°F. Set the salmon on an oiled baking sheet, season with salt and pepper, and drizzle with the vinaigrette. Allow to marinate for 15 minutes. Set in the oven and bake for 9 to 12 minutes or until almost opaque all the way through.

Cut the avocados in half lengthwise and remove the pit. Scoop the flesh into a medium bowl. Using a fork, coarsely mash the avocado with the lime juice and olive oil. Season with salt and pepper to taste.

To serve, divide the salmon, taco shells, and black beans among the plates. Pass around the avocado smash, vinaigrette, tomatoes, jalapeños, onions, scallions, queso fresco, cilantro, and hot sauce at the table, allowing guests to build their own tacos.

BLACK BEANS

2 cups dried black beans (see Notes)
6 cups cold water
1 bay leaf
1 onion, quartered
1 tsp sea salt

JALAPEÑO VINAIGRETTE

1 jalapeño
Zest and juice of 3 limes
2 Tbsp Dijon mustard
1½ tsp white wine vinegar
½ tsp sea salt
1 cup canola oil

TACO SHELLS

16 (4- to 5-inch) soft corn tortillas
1 cup grated mozzarella

SALMON TACOS

1 lb pink salmon fillets
Sea salt and coarsely ground black pepper
½ cup Jalapeño Vinaigrette (see above)
2 ripe avocados
2 Tbsp lime juice
1 Tbsp extra-virgin olive oil
1 cup diced tomatoes
2 to 3 jalapeños, sliced
1 white onion, chopped
4 scallions, chopped
2 cups queso fresco (fresh cheese), crumbled
½ cup fresh cilantro leaves
Mexican-style hot sauce such as Tapatío or Valentina Salsa Picante

1 lb Brussels sprouts, trimmed
2 Tbsp olive oil
Sea salt and coarsely ground black pepper
4 (4 to 5 oz) skin-on steelhead fillets
Lemon Vinaigrette (page 77)
4 cups torn radicchio leaves
1 cup shaved Parmesan
Zest of 1 lemon

Steelhead, a freshwater fish with terrific natural fats, is very forgiving, so it's the perfect species to start with if you're new to cooking with fish. Here it's simply baked, then served with a salad of radicchio, shaved Parmesan, and the outer leaves of Brussels sprouts, blanched until tender-crisp, plus the delicate inner hearts, roasted until sweet, crunchy, and golden.

STEELHEAD WITH BRUSSELS SPROUT SALAD

Preheat the oven to 400°F. Remove any limp and broken outer leaves from the Brussels sprouts and discard. Remove and reserve a few more layers of leaves from each sprout until just the tightly wrapped center remains. Cut the sprouts in half.

Toss the Brussels sprouts with olive oil on a baking sheet. Season with salt and pepper. Roast for 20 to 30 minutes or until golden brown and crispy. (The darker the caramelization, the better—just don't let them burn as they'll turn bitter.)

Meanwhile, bring a pot of salted water to a boil over high heat, and set a bowl of ice water nearby. Add the reserved Brussels sprout leaves to the boiling water, and blanch for 30 seconds or until just tender. Use a slotted spoon to transfer immediately to the ice water to stop the cooking and set the bright green color and crunchy texture. When completely cool, drain and pat dry with paper towels.

Preheat the oven again to 400°F. Line a baking sheet with parchment paper. Use paper towels to pat the fish dry, and season with salt and pepper. Set on the baking sheet skin side down, and drizzle with a little of the lemon vinaigrette. Bake for 10 to 12 minutes or until almost opaque all the way through.

In a large serving bowl, mix together the radicchio leaves, roasted Brussels sprouts, blanched Brussels sprout leaves, and shaved Parmesan. Toss with just enough vinaigrette to coat, and season with salt and pepper to taste. Add the lemon zest.

To serve, divide the salad among plates and set a fillet alongside.

This dish is a summertime celebration of land and sea—when fresh salmon is at its peak from late July to August, and backyard gardens and farmers' markets are bursting with an abundance of squash and greens. For the pesto, select an aged and crumbly farmhouse cheese with sharp bite.

SERVES 4

GRILLED WILD SALMON AND SUMMER SQUASH SALAD WITH ZUCCHINI PESTO AND LEMON VINAIGRETTE

ZUCCHINI PESTO Heat a small skillet over medium-low heat. Add the pine nuts and toast, stirring frequently, for 3 to 5 minutes or until golden brown. Transfer to a plate.

Slice the zucchini lengthwise and scoop out the seeds with a spoon. Roughly chop, or grate on the large holes of a box grater.

Combine the pine nuts, zucchini, and remaining ingredients in a blender or food processor and blend to your desired consistency. (I like it to have a bit of texture. In fact, if you grate the zucchini, you can skip the blender and just combine the ingredients in a bowl for a rustic pesto.) Taste and adjust seasoning if desired.

LEMON VINAIGRETTE Combine the lemon zest and juice, mustard, honey, and salt in a small bowl. While whisking, slowly drizzle the oil in a thin steady stream until incorporated and the mixture is emulsified. Adjust seasoning to taste. (Alternatively, you can do this with an immersion blender or in a blender or small food processor.) Can be made ahead of time; will keep refrigerated for up to 2 weeks (although the lemon flavor will start to weaken after a few days).

SALMON AND SUMMER SQUASH Preheat the grill to medium-high. Clean and oil the cooking grate. If you have pattypan or round zucchini, cut into wedges. For small yellow summer squash or zucchini, slice in half lengthwise. Larger squash can be halved crosswise and then sliced into quarters lengthwise. Toss the vegetables with 2 tablespoons of the oil in a medium bowl. Season with salt and pepper to taste.

Set the vegetables on the grate and grill (covered if using gas) until brown grill marks appear, about 5 minutes. Turn and cook for another 5 minutes or until tender. (If vegetables are browning too quickly before they are tender, move to an area of indirect heat.) Transfer to a plate.

Use paper towels to pat the fish dry. Brush both sides with the remaining tablespoon of oil, and season with salt and pepper. Oil the grate. Lay the fish on the grill skin side down. Cook for 3 minutes or until a golden crust forms on the skin. Use a spatula to turn over, and cook for another 3 to 4 minutes or until almost opaque all the way through.

To serve, toss the lettuce with just enough vinaigrette to coat. Season with salt and pepper to taste. Divide among plates and set the salmon on top. Arrange the squash around the fish. Spoon pesto on the salmon and squash. Sprinkle reserved pine nuts over all and garnish with some grated cheese.

ZUCCHINI PESTO
¼ cup pine nuts, plus extra for garnish
1 zucchini
1 small clove garlic (optional)
¼ cup grated aged Gouda or cheddar, plus extra for garnish
Zest and juice of ½ lemon
1½ Tbsp extra-virgin olive oil
Sea salt and coarsely ground black pepper

LEMON VINAIGRETTE
Zest and juice of 1 lemon
1 Tbsp Dijon mustard
¾ tsp honey
½ tsp sea salt
½ cup canola oil

SALMON AND SUMMER SQUASH
2 lb summer squash in a variety of shapes, sizes, and colors
3 Tbsp canola oil (divided)
Sea salt and coarsely ground black pepper
4 (4 to 5 oz) skin-on salmon fillets
8 cups torn butter lettuce or salad greens

Salmon makes dinnertime so easy. Its full flavor means it can stand alone with minimal seasoning, or stand up to just about any assertive ingredients you crave, including kale tossed with an autumnal cider vinaigrette. To help satisfy our hunger for this fish without depleting the ocean, the 'Namgis First Nation of Vancouver, BC, has made tremendous strides in sustainably farming Atlantic salmon. Their landlocked pens at the north end of Vancouver Island ensure the fish never escape into the ocean where they might wreak havoc on wild populations. In the States, farmed steelhead or arctic char offers a similarly sustainable alternative with a comparable flavor and nutritional profile.

HONEY AND APPLE CIDER VINAIGRETTE

1½ Tbsp apple cider vinegar
2 tsp Dijon mustard
1 Tbsp honey
½ tsp sea salt
⅔ cup canola oil

SALAD

6 cups torn purple, red
  Russian, or curly leaf
  kale (stems removed)
4 (4 to 5 oz) skin-on Kuterra
  farmed salmon or
  steelhead fillets
Sea salt and coarsely
  ground black pepper
1 Tbsp canola oil
2 Tbsp unsalted butter
1 lemon, halved
6 cups torn baby kale
1 large tart-sweet apple
  such as Honeycrisp,
  unpeeled, cored, and
  thinly sliced
1 cup toasted hazelnuts
1 cup fromage frais or fresh
  whole-milk ricotta
½ cup dried cranberries

SERVES 4

SALMON AND KALE SALAD WITH APPLES, DRIED CRANBERRIES, HAZELNUTS, AND FROMAGE FRAIS

HONEY AND APPLE CIDER VINAIGRETTE
Combine the vinegar, mustard, honey, and salt in a small bowl. While whisking, slowly drizzle the oil in a thin steady stream until incorporated and the mixture is emulsified. Adjust seasoning to taste. (Alternatively, you can do this with an immersion blender or in a blender or small food processor.) Can be made ahead of time; will keep refrigerated for up to 2 weeks.

SALAD Bring a large pot of salted water to a boil over high heat. Set a large bowl of ice water nearby. Add the purple, red Russian, or curly leaf kale to the boiling water and blanch for 45 seconds. Use tongs or a slotted spoon to transfer immediately to the ice water. When completely cool, drain, squeezing out the excess water.

Use paper towels to pat the fish dry, and season with salt and pepper. Heat the oil in a heavy-bottomed skillet over medium-high heat until almost smoking. Carefully lay the fish in the pan skin side down. (If necessary, cook the fish in batches to prevent overcrowding, which will keep the fish from caramelizing properly.) Reduce the heat to medium and cook for 3 minutes; a golden crust will have formed on the skin. Flip the fillets over, skin side up, and cook for another 3 minutes or until flesh is browned, and fish is almost opaque all the way through and flakes easily. Add the butter to the pan. Allow it to melt while you squeeze the lemon over the fish. Use a spoon to baste each fillet with the buttery juices for about 1 minute. Transfer the fish to a plate and keep warm.

In a large bowl, toss the blanched kale and baby kale with just enough vinaigrette to coat. Season with salt and pepper to taste. Divide between 4 plates and garnish with the apples, hazelnuts, fromage frais (or ricotta), and cranberries. Top with the pan-seared salmon and drizzle with a little more vinaigrette. Serve warm.

Bouillabaisse—a fisherman's stew from Marseilles— was traditionally built around whatever was pulled up in the nets and traps that day. The fishers would sell their catch in neat fillets, then toss all the trimmings and bycatch, along with some shellfish, into a broth infused with aromatics such as fennel and garlic. Just about any firm white fish or shellfish would be delicious in this tomato-based broth. You can keep it simple with just halibut and clams or follow in the fishermen's footsteps and add a little of everything.

SERVES 6

WEST COAST BOUILLABAISSE

Heat the oil in a large pot over medium-high heat. Add the fennel, onions, celery, carrots, and bell peppers. Sauté for 5 minutes or until onions are tender and translucent. Add the garlic and sauté for another minute. Add the wine and stir to scrape up the browned bits. Pour in the Caesar mix (or tomato juice and clam juice), fish stock (or vegetable stock), chili flakes, fennel seeds, and bay leaves. Bring to a boil over high heat, reduce to medium-low, and simmer for 30 minutes or until the vegetables are tender and flavors are more concentrated.

Heat the canola oil in a heavy-bottomed skillet over medium-high heat. Pat-dry the scallops and add to the pan. Allow to sear undisturbed for about 2 minutes or until browned. Season with salt and pepper, flip the scallops over, and sear for another 2 minutes. Add the butter and baste. Transfer to a plate.

When ready to serve, add the clams and mussels to the broth. Cover and cook until they just begin to open, about 3 minutes. Add the fish and mixed shellfish. Cover and cook another 3 to 5 minutes or until shells are fully open and fish is cooked through. (Discard any clams or mussels that haven't opened.) Stir in the scallops.

Divide soup among bowls, or serve family style from the cooking pot or a warmed tureen. Sprinkle each bowl with fennel fronds, celery leaves, scallions, chives, and chili flakes. Top with 1 tablespoon chili mayo. Serve with crusty bread and lemon wedges on the side.

1 Tbsp extra-virgin olive oil
1 bulb fennel, sliced and fronds reserved for garnish
1 small red onion, sliced
2 stalks celery, sliced
2 carrots, sliced
1 yellow, red, or orange bell pepper, sliced
6 cloves garlic, finely sliced
1 cup dry white wine
4 cups Walter Caesar Mix (or 3 cups tomato juice and 1 cup clam juice)
4 cups Fish Stock (page 90) or Vegetable Stock (page 138)
1 Tbsp chili flakes, plus extra for garnish
1 Tbsp fennel seeds
2 bay leaves
2 Tbsp canola oil
6 scallops
Sea salt and coarsely ground black pepper
2 Tbsp unsalted butter
½ lb live clams, scrubbed
½ lb live mussels, scrubbed and debearded
2 lb skinless firm fish fillets such as halibut, salmon, or lingcod, cut into 1-inch cubes
½ lb mixed shellfish such as peeled and deveined shrimp and/or crabmeat
Tender celery leaves, for garnish
4 scallions, chopped, for garnish
Chopped fresh chives, for garnish
6 Tbsp Smoked Chili Mayo (page 116), to serve
Crusty bread, to serve
Lemon wedges, to serve

BLACK PEPPER VINAIGRETTE

Zest and juice of 1 lemon

1 Tbsp Dijon mustard

¾ tsp honey

¼ tsp sea salt

¾ tsp coarsely ground black pepper

½ cup canola oil

BEETS THREE WAYS

2 lb medium beets (preferably a mixture of red, golden, and Chioggia), with greens attached (divided)

3 Tbsp extra-virgin olive oil (divided)

Sea salt and coarsely ground black pepper

1 Tbsp unsalted butter

SERVES 4

SALMON WITH BEETS THREE WAYS AND BLACK PEPPER VINAIGRETTE

BLACK PEPPER VINAIGRETTE Combine the lemon zest and juice, mustard, honey, and salt and pepper in a small bowl. While whisking, slowly drizzle the oil in a thin steady stream until incorporated and the mixture is emulsified. Adjust seasoning to taste. (Alternatively, you can do this with an immersion blender or in a blender or small food processor.) Can be made ahead of time; will keep refrigerated for up to 2 weeks (although the lemon flavor will start to weaken after a few days).

BEETS THREE WAYS Preheat the oven to 400°F. Bring a medium saucepan of water to a boil and salt generously.

Cut the greens from the beets and reserve. Remove the thin root end and discard. Peel the beets with a vegetable peeler. Set aside one raw peeled beet (preferably a striped Chioggia) for garnish. Dice the rest into ¾-inch cubes.

Toss half the diced beets (preferably golden or Chioggia) with 1 tablespoon olive oil and salt and pepper and spread in an even layer on a rimmed baking sheet. Roast for about 30 minutes, stirring once halfway through, until beets are easily pierced with a fork.

Add the remaining diced beets (preferably red) to the boiling water. Cook until tender, about 25 minutes. Transfer to a blender or food processor. Add the remaining 2 tablespoons olive oil, and puree until smooth. Season to taste with salt and pepper.

Wash the beet greens well. Separate the stems from the leaves and roughly chop the stems. Heat the butter in a large skillet over medium heat, add the stems, and sauté for 5 minutes or until tender. Add the greens and sauté for another few minutes or until wilted. Season with salt and pepper to taste.

SALMON
4 (4 to 5 oz) skin-on salmon
   (or lingcod or sablefish)
   fillets
Sea salt and coarsely
   ground black pepper
1 Tbsp canola oil
2 Tbsp unsalted butter
1 lemon, halved

SALMON Preheat the oven to 400°F. Use paper towels to pat the fish dry, and season with salt and pepper. Heat the oil in a heavy-bottomed, ovenproof skillet over medium-high heat until almost smoking. Carefully lay the fish in the pan skin side down. (If necessary, cook the fish in batches to prevent overcrowding, which will keep the fish from caramelizing properly.) Reduce the heat to medium and cook for 1 minute or until a golden crust forms on the skin. Flip the fillets over, skin side up, and cook for another 2 to 3 minutes or until browned. Place the pan in the oven and roast for 3 to 4 minutes or until fish is opaque in the center and flakes easily.

Remove from the oven and add the butter to the pan. Allow it to melt while you squeeze the lemon over the fish. Use a spoon to baste each fillet with the buttery juices for about 1 minute. Transfer to a plate.

To serve, spread the beet puree on each plate, add the roasted beets and the beet greens, and place the salmon on top. Thinly slice the reserved raw peeled beet on a mandoline and set a few slices on each fillet. Drizzle a tablespoon or two of the vinaigrette over all.

Quintessentially West Coast, planking pays homage to the First Nations peoples of North America, who were cooking salmon on wood planks over an open fire long before Europeans arrived. It's an ingenious way to impart earthy, smoky, and even floral notes to the fish, depending on the type of wood you use. Although cedar is a classic choice, alder and oak work beautifully with salmon, too. You can find grilling planks at gourmet retailers, or go the DIY route with untreated wood from the hardware store. Look for 1-inch-thick and 8-inch-wide pieces, and have them cut 8 to 12 inches long. Just be sure to give them a good sanding first to remove splinters and allow time to soak them before using.

SERVES 4

1 (1½ lb) skin-on salmon fillet, cut into 4 portions
Extra-virgin olive oil
Sea salt and coarsely ground black pepper
4 sprigs thyme, leaves only, plus extra for garnish (divided)
4 nectarines or apricots, halved
2 Tbsp honey
4 oz (½ cup) fresh whole-milk ricotta
Sliced toasted almonds, for garnish
Garden salad, to serve

PLANKED WILD SALMON WITH NECTARINES, THYME, HONEY, ALMONDS, AND RICOTTA

Soak the cedar plank in water for at least 30 minutes and up to a day before using.

Preheat the grill to medium (about 350°F). Use paper towels to pat the fish dry. Rub all over with olive oil, and season both sides with salt and pepper. Sprinkle the thyme leaves over the salmon (leaving some for the nectarines and for the garnish), and press to adhere.

Put the plank on the grill directly over the flames. Cover the grill and allow the plank to heat until starting to just smoke, about 2 minutes. Turn and repeat on the other side. Add the fish skin side down to the plank. Add the nectarines cut side up. Drizzle the nectarines with honey, sprinkle with most of the remaining thyme leaves, and a little salt. Cover the grill and cook for 7 to 12 minutes

or until fish is almost opaque all the way through and flakes easily and the nectarines are caramelized and tender. (If the plank gets too hot and ignites, spritz it with water from a spray bottle. Alternatively, you can grill the salmon directly on an oiled grill grate for 3 to 4 minutes per side, and roast the nectarines in a baking dish in a 400°F oven for 12 minutes.)

To serve, add a couple tablespoons of ricotta over each piece of fish, and sprinkle with the almonds. Garnish with thyme. Serve with a garden salad.

Classic pesto is usually made with basil and toasted pine nuts, but here I've gone with hearty kale, whose mild bitterness is offset by the gentle sweetness of cashews. (Jar some of this delicious green paste to use with any firm fish, such as rockfish, albacore tuna, or sturgeon.) For the tomato jam and confit, reach for the sweetest heirloom cherry tomatoes you can find. Sweet 100 and Sun Gold are two of my favorite choices.

HEIRLOOM TOMATO JAM AND CONFIT

3 pints (about 7 cups) heirloom-style cherry tomatoes (divided)
½ cup water
¼ cup white wine vinegar
¼ cup honey
1 Tbsp sea salt
1 tsp coarsely ground black pepper
1 cup olive oil
1 sprig rosemary
2 cloves garlic, thinly sliced

KALE CASHEW PESTO

½ bunch kale, stems removed and leaves torn (about 3 cups)
6 cups spinach leaves
3 Tbsp extra-virgin olive oil
½ cup toasted cashews
½ cup hot water
3 Tbsp Parmesan
1 tsp sea salt
1 tsp coarsely ground black pepper

SALMON

4 (4 to 5 oz) skinless salmon fillets
Sea salt and coarsely ground black pepper
1 Tbsp canola oil
2 Tbsp unsalted butter
1 lemon, halved
Chopped toasted cashews, for garnish

WILD SALMON WITH HEIRLOOM TOMATO JAM AND KALE CASHEW PESTO

HEIRLOOM TOMATO JAM AND CONFIT For the tomato jam, in a medium saucepan combine 4 cups of the tomatoes, water, vinegar, honey, and salt and pepper. Bring to a boil over high heat, reduce to medium-low, and simmer for 20 minutes or until the tomatoes are softened and cooked through. Transfer the mixture to a blender and puree until smooth.

For the tomato confit, in the same saucepan combine the remaining 3 cups tomatoes, olive oil, rosemary, and garlic. Bring to a simmer over medium-high heat, reduce to low, and gently cook for 15 to 20 minutes or until tomatoes just start to lose their skins. Remove and discard the rosemary.

KALE CASHEW PESTO Bring a large pot of salted water to a boil over high heat. Set a large bowl of ice water nearby. Add the kale and spinach to the boiling water, and blanch for 45 seconds. Use tongs or a slotted spoon to transfer immediately to the ice water. When completely cool, drain.

In a blender, combine the blanched greens, olive oil, cashews, hot water, Parmesan, and salt and pepper, and puree until smooth.

SALMON Preheat the oven to 400°F. Use paper towels to pat the fish dry, and season with salt and pepper. Heat the oil in a heavy-bottomed, ovenproof skillet over medium-high heat until almost smoking. Carefully lay the fish in the pan. (If necessary, cook the fish in batches to prevent overcrowding, which will keep the fish from caramelizing properly.) Reduce the heat to medium and cook for 1 minute or until a golden crust forms on the flesh. Flip the fillets over and cook for another 2 to 3 minutes or until browned. Place the pan in the oven and roast for 3 to 4 minutes or until fish is opaque in the center and flakes easily.

Remove from the oven and add the butter to the pan. Allow it to melt while you squeeze the lemon over the fish. Use a spoon to baste each fillet with the buttery juices for about 1 minute. Transfer the fish to a plate.

Spoon the tomato jam onto each plate, add the salmon, and top with a spoonful of pesto and tomato confit. Garnish with the cashews.

One of my fondest childhood memories is baking a whole salmon that my dad and I had caught just outside of our house on the shore in Sydney, BC. There's just something so primal about cooking a whole fish—head to tail—especially when you've caught it yourself. But even if you've picked it up from the store, when you present a whole fish, or even a whole fish fillet, at the table, it's the kind of dramatic gesture that guests love. For this party-ready dish, I keep the preparation simple and let the sauce vierge do the talking. Uncooked and loaded with herbs, this classic French sauce is brighter than the usual creamy sauces we associate with French cuisine. It's a stunner with salmon but delicious with tuna, too.

SERVES 8

WILD SALMON BAKE WITH SAUCE VIERGE

SAUCE VIERGE Combine all the ingredients in a large bowl. Season to taste. Set aside to marinate for 30 minutes.

SALMON Preheat the oven to 350°F. Line a baking sheet with parchment paper. Brush the skin of the salmon with olive oil and season both sides with salt and pepper.

Place the salmon skin side down onto the prepared baking sheet. Add the lemon cut side up beside the salmon, and bake for about 20 minutes, depending on the thickness of fish. An instant-read thermometer inserted in the thickest part should read 120°F to 125°F. Set aside to rest for 2 to 3 minutes.

Add a few generous spoonfuls of sauce vierge on top, drizzle with olive oil, and serve with the charred lemon.

CHEF'S NOTES: Alternatively, preheat the grill and cook on the grate skin side down. (The BBQ acts like an "oven" with the lid closed so you cook the fish evenly.)

SAUCE VIERGE
4 Roma tomatoes, seeded and diced (about 3 cups)
1 large shallot, finely chopped (about ¼ cup)
½ cup chopped flat-leaf parsley
½ cup chopped fresh chives
3 Tbsp chopped fresh tarragon
½ cup extra-virgin olive oil
Zest and juice of 1 large lemon
Sea salt and coarsely ground black pepper

SALMON
1 (2 to 3 lb) salmon fillet
Olive oil, for brushing the salmon and for drizzling
Sea salt and coarsely ground black pepper
½ lemon

This Spanish classic is a healthful, comforting, and easy one-pot dish. But best of all, it's an artful display of seafood, guaranteed to wow company. Paella will happily accommodate just about any shellfish. You can splurge and garnish it with Dungeness crabmeat and seared scallops, or go the economical route and stick with clams and mussels. Traditionally, short-grained Bomba rice is used to make this dish (and arborio is a common substitute), but I prefer a seven-grain rice for its diverse textures and nutty flavors.

FISH STOCK

3 lb white fish bones and heads
1 bulb fennel, including the stalks, chopped
1 white onion, chopped
2 stalks celery, chopped
1 head garlic, sliced in half horizontally
1 bay leaf
1 Tbsp sea salt
1 Tbsp black peppercorns
1 tsp chili flakes
6 cups cold water

PAELLA

4 cups Fish Stock (see above)
1 to 2 cups tomato juice
2 Tbsp canola oil (divided)
1 lb firm fish fillets, such as salmon or halibut, cut into bite-size pieces
Sea salt and coarsely ground black pepper, to taste
1 red onion, finely chopped
3 cloves garlic, finely chopped
1 yellow bell pepper, finely chopped
1 red bell pepper, finely chopped
2 Roma tomatoes, seeded and diced
2 cups 7-grain, Bomba, or arborio rice
12 live clams (about 1¼ lb), scrubbed
12 live mussels (about ½ lb), scrubbed and debearded
1 lb wild shrimp or prawns, unpeeled
6 cooked scallops

GARNISH

¼ cup finely chopped fresh chives or scallions
1 tomato, seeded and chopped
Flaked sea salt
1 tsp fennel pollen (see Notes on page 51)
2 Tbsp olive oil
Juice of ½ small lemon

SERVES 6

PACIFIC PAELLA

FISH STOCK Place the fish bones and heads in a large bowl (if necessary, cut to fit) and rinse well with cold water.

In a large stockpot, combine the fish bones and heads, fennel, onion, celery, garlic halves, bay leaf, salt, peppercorns, and chili flakes. Add the water and bring to a simmer over high heat. Reduce the heat to low and cook uncovered for 45 minutes, skimming off any foam that rises to the surface. Set aside to cool, then strain and use immediately or refrigerate for up to 48 hours. You should have about 4 cups.

PAELLA Bring the fish stock and 1 cup tomato juice to a simmer in a medium saucepan set over medium-high heat. Reduce to low and keep warm.

Meanwhile, heat 1 tablespoon of the olive oil in a 12-inch paella pan or sauté pan over medium-high heat. Season the fish with salt and pepper and sauté until lightly browned, about 1 minute (it won't be cooked through). Transfer to a plate.

Heat the remaining tablespoon of oil in the pan over medium heat. Add the onions and sauté for 7 minutes or until translucent. Add the garlic and sauté for another minute.

Add both peppers and cook until softened. Add the tomatoes, and salt and pepper to taste. Cook until all liquid has been released.

Add the rice and cook, stirring, for 2 minutes. Stir in the warm fish stock and tomato juice mixture. Season with salt and pepper to taste. Bring to a boil over medium-high heat, then reduce to low. Cook, uncovered, for 10 minutes. Gently nestle the fish, clams, and mussels into the rice and arrange the shrimp on top. Continue cooking for 10 minutes, without stirring, until the clams and mussels open up (discard any that don't open), the liquid is absorbed, and the rice is tender. (Add a little hot stock or tomato juice if the rice seems too dry.)

When the paella is done, turn up the heat to medium-high and cook for about 45 seconds to toast the rice on the bottom and create what's called the socarrat. Remove the pan from the heat. Cover the pan with aluminum foil. Add the scallops and let stand 10 minutes before serving.

Garnish the paella with the chives (or scallions) and tomatoes. Sprinkle with flaked sea salt and fennel pollen. Mix together the olive oil and lemon juice and drizzle over the rice. Serve with a simple side green salad.

CHERRY BALSAMIC SAUCE

1 lb Bing cherries, pitted (divided)
1 cup cherry juice
2 Tbsp light brown sugar
½ cup balsamic vinegar
Sea salt and coarsely ground black pepper

SALMON

1 (1½ lb) salmon fillet
Olive oil, for brushing the salmon and for drizzling
½ lemon
Sea salt and coarsely ground black pepper

SERVES 4 TO 6

BAKED SALMON WITH CHERRY BALSAMIC SAUCE

CHERRY BALSAMIC SAUCE In a large saucepan, combine two-thirds of the cherries, the cherry juice, sugar, vinegar, and a pinch of salt and pepper. Bring to a boil over high heat, reduce heat to medium, and simmer for 25 minutes or until sauce has reduced by about half. Meanwhile, halve the remaining one-third of the cherries. Add them to the pan, and cook for another 5 minutes. Remove the pan from the heat, season to taste with additional salt and pepper, and set aside.

SALMON Preheat oven to 350°F. Line a baking sheet with parchment paper. Brush the skin of the salmon with olive oil and season both sides with salt and pepper.

Place the salmon, skin side down, onto the prepared baking sheet. Squeeze lemon juice over fish, and bake until fish flakes easily, about 20 minutes, depending on the thickness of fish. An instant-read thermometer inserted in the thickest part should read 120°F to 125°F.

To serve, spoon the sauce over top of the salmon and enjoy!

This dish is an explosion of contrasting flavors and a last hurrah for the end of summer. Charring scallions brings out their gentler side. Just bear in mind that there's a fine line between charred and burnt: you don't want them to taste acrid, but rather sweetened, and they should take on a pleasing deep-golden-brown color, not turn to charcoal. Be sure to get clean grill lines on your peaches by leaving them directly on the grill in one spot without peeking or fussing before they've had time to take on good color.

SERVES 6

GRILLED SALMON WITH CHEESY AND SPICY CORN, MAPLE-GRILLED PEACHES, AND CHARRED SCALLIONS

SPICY CORN Bring a saucepan of water to a boil over high heat (no need to add salt). Break the cobs in half and add to the water. Reduce the heat to medium and simmer, covered, for 20 minutes. Strain and reserve the corn stock.

Heat the oil in a large skillet over medium heat, add the shallots, and sauté for 5 minutes or until tender and translucent. Add the garlic and sauté until fragrant. Stir in the corn kernels and ½ cup corn stock (refrigerate the rest of the corn stock for use in soups or chowder). Simmer for 10 minutes or until the kernels are cooked and liquid has reduced. Stir in both cheeses and the jalapeño, and season with salt and pepper.

GRILLED PEACHES AND SCALLIONS Preheat the grill to medium-high. Clean and oil the cooking grate. In a bowl, gently toss the peaches with 2 tablespoons of the olive oil, smoked paprika, and salt and pepper until well coated. Place the peach wedges on the grate, and grill without disturbing until lightly charred, about 2 minutes per side. Transfer to a platter and drizzle with the maple syrup.

In a bowl, toss the scallions with the remaining 2 tablespoons of olive oil, and season with salt and pepper. Grill perpendicular to the cooking grate until charred and golden brown, 1 to 2 minutes per side. (Alternatively, you can broil the peaches and scallions on a baking sheet under the broiler.) Transfer scallions to the platter with the peaches.

GRILLED SALMON Preheat the grill to medium-high. Clean and oil the cooking grate. Use paper towels to pat the fish dry. Brush both sides with the olive oil, and season with salt and pepper. Lay the fish on the grill skin side down. Cook for 3 minutes or until a golden crust forms on the skin and the fish releases easily from the grate. Use a spatula to turn over, and cook the other side for another 3 to 4 minutes or until almost opaque all the way through.

To serve, divide the salmon, grilled peaches and scallions, and spicy corn among plates.

SPICY CORN

6 ears of fresh corn, kernels removed and cobs reserved
1 Tbsp canola oil
1 shallot, finely chopped
1 garlic clove, finely chopped
1 cup grated aged white cheddar
½ cup mascarpone
1 small jalapeño, seeded and finely chopped
Sea salt and coarsely ground black pepper

GRILLED PEACHES AND SCALLIONS

3 ripe peaches, each cut into 6 wedges
¼ cup olive oil (divided)
1 tsp smoked paprika
Sea salt and coarsely ground black pepper
2 Tbsp maple syrup
18 scallions, white and light green parts only, trimmed

GRILLED SALMON

6 (4 to 5 oz) skin-on salmon fillets or steaks
2 Tbsp olive oil
Sea salt and coarsely ground black pepper

Foolproof, elegantly impressive, and blessedly mess free, cooking en papillote *is a busy cook's get-out-of-jail-free card. With the exception of the densest fish species, such as sturgeon or lingcod, all fish take well to this cooking method, and it's so easy to customize each diner's little parchment-paper packet. Here rich steelhead is simply flavored with a little butter, lemon, and herbs, and then served with a sweet-tart compote of apples and raisins. But you can change things up with different herbs or spices, and even thinly sliced or shaved vegetables that will cook with the fish right in the pouch.*

SERVES 4

STEELHEAD EN PAPILLOTE WITH GOLDEN RAISIN AND APPLE COMPOTE

GOLDEN RAISIN AND APPLE COMPOTE

2 cups golden raisins
2 cups apple juice
½ cup apple cider vinegar
¼ cup honey
1 tsp sea salt
1 Granny Smith apple, unpeeled

STEELHEAD

½ cup pine nuts (divided)
4 (4 to 5 oz) steelhead steaks
Sea salt and coarsely ground black pepper
¼ cup (½ stick) unsalted butter
¼ cup chopped fresh flat-leaf parsley or chives
1 lemon, thinly sliced
Roasted root vegetables such as parsnips or celery root, to serve

GOLDEN RAISIN AND APPLE COMPOTE Combine the raisins, apple juice, vinegar, honey, and salt in a medium saucepan, and bring to a boil over high heat. Reduce the heat to low and simmer for 15 minutes or until raisins are plump and the liquid is reduced to one-quarter of the original volume. Remove the pan from the heat.

Core the apple, then dice into pieces about the same size as the raisins. Stir the apples into the saucepan. Set aside to cool.

STEELHEAD Preheat the oven to 350°F. Spread the pine nuts on a rimmed baking sheet and toast, stirring occasionally, for 5 to 10 minutes or until golden. Remove and set aside to cool. (Alternatively, you can toast them, stirring frequently, in a dry skillet over medium-low heat for 3 to 5 minutes.) Stir in ¼ cup of pine nuts into the compote.

Increase the oven temperature to 400°F. Fold 4 (18-inch-long) pieces of parchment paper in half. Place each fillet on one side of each paper. Season with salt and pepper. Dot each fillet with a tablespoon of butter, and sprinkle with a tablespoon of parsley (or chives). Set 1 or 2 lemon slices on top. Fold the paper over the salmon and double fold around all edges to completely seal the fish. Set parchment packets on a baking sheet and bake for 12 minutes or until the flesh is almost opaque all the way through and flakes easily.

To serve, transfer each pouch to a plate. Cut the tops of the pouches to open them up, and add a generous spoonful of the compote to each fillet. Garnish each with 1 Tbsp toasted pine nuts and serve with a side of root vegetables.

This dish sits at the intersection between soul food and spa food. Full-flavored Kuterra salmon is coated in a glaze that brings together the earthy, umami flavor of red miso and the toasty notes of maple syrup. The fish is served on a bed of warm and sticky sushi rice. To me, a perfectly executed bowl of rice is extraordinarily satisfying in its own right, and here in this recipe, it's as much of a treat as the seafood. A great dish is not about fussy or obscure ingredients and techniques—it's about getting simple things right and bringing them together harmoniously.

MISO MAPLE GLAZE

½ cup canola oil
2 Tbsp red miso paste (yellow works too)
2 Tbsp maple syrup or honey
2 Tbsp rice wine vinegar

SUSHI RICE

2 cups Japanese sushi rice
2 cups cold water, for cooking the rice
2 Tbsp seasoned rice wine vinegar

SALMON

4 (4 to 5 oz) skin-on Kuterra farmed salmon or steelhead fillets
Sea salt and coarsely ground black pepper
1 Tbsp canola oil
2 Tbsp Miso Maple Glaze (see above)
1 lime, halved
1 Tbsp toasted sesame seeds, for garnish
2 scallions, chopped, for garnish
1 Tbsp chopped nori, for garnish

SERVES 4

SALMON WITH SUSHI RICE AND MISO MAPLE GLAZE

MISO MAPLE GLAZE Combine all the ingredients in a blender, or a deep bowl with an immersion blender, and blend until emulsified. (You'll make more than you need; the glaze will keep refrigerated for several weeks.)

SUSHI RICE Rinse the rice in several changes of water until the water is clear. In a saucepan, combine the rice with the water, and bring to a boil over high heat. Reduce to low, cover, and cook for 15 minutes or until the liquid is absorbed. Remove the pan from the heat and let stand for 15 minutes.

Transfer the rice to a large mixing bowl, and sprinkle with half the vinegar. Stir the rice and sprinkle more of the vinegar, a little at a time while turning the rice over to ensure all the rice gets coated. Keep warm.

SALMON Use paper towels to pat the fish dry, and season with salt and pepper. Heat the oil in a heavy-bottomed skillet over medium-high heat until almost smoking. Carefully lay the fish in the pan skin side down. (If necessary, cook the fish in batches to prevent overcrowding, which will keep the fish from caramelizing properly.) Reduce the heat to medium, and cook for 2 minutes or until a golden crust forms on the skin. Flip the fillets over, skin side up, and add the miso-maple glaze to the pan. Squeeze the lime over each fillet. Cook, basting with the pan juices, for another 3 to 4 minutes or until fish is browned and almost opaque all the way through.

To serve, divide the sushi rice among shallow bowls or plates. Set a fillet on top of rice and garnish with sesame seeds, scallions, and chopped nori.

Oily fish such as sardines are often relegated to supporting roles in seafood dishes, but they are packed with flavor and made for stardom. Bold and oily sardines require complements that will hold their own and provide extra depth. I always have preserved lemons in my fridge for the simple fact they add deep, and somewhat funky and floral lemony flavor to seafood recipes. Although they take minutes to prepare, it'll be at least a month before you can use them. In a pinch, you can buy preserved lemons from gourmet grocers or in the ethnic foods aisle.

SERVES 4

PRESERVED LEMONS
8 lemons
1 cup kosher salt
Juice of 1 to 2 lemons
1 sterilized mason jar

SARDINES
12 fresh sardines, anchovies, or herring (see Notes)
3 Tbsp extra-virgin olive oil (divided), plus extra for drizzling
Sea salt and coarsely ground black pepper
2 preserved lemons, flesh discarded, rind finely chopped
½ cup chopped fresh chives or basil, or a mix of both
2 scallions, thinly sliced
1 head butter lettuce, leaves separated
Flaked sea salt, to sprinkle
1 lemon, cut into wedges, to serve

SARDINES WITH PRESERVED LEMONS, HERBS, AND BUTTER LETTUCE

PRESERVED LEMONS Cut the lemons lengthwise in quarters but not all the way through. Put them in a bowl and generously rub and pack the crevices with the salt. Layer the lemons and more salt in the jar, packing them as tightly as possible. Add enough lemon juice to ensure they're completely submerged in liquid. Screw on the lid and store in the refrigerator for at least 1 month before using. (Lemons will keep, refrigerated, up to 6 months. The bold flavor develops over time.)

SARDINES Preheat the grill to high heat. Clean and oil the cooking grate. (If brining, remove the fish from the brine and pat dry with paper towels.) Rub all over with 1 tablespoon of the oil, and season inside and out with salt and pepper. Set the fish on the grate and grill for 1 to 2 minutes per side or until the skin is browned and the flesh flakes easily. (Alternatively, you can broil the sardines on a baking sheet set just under the broiler for the same amount of time.)

In a small bowl, mix together the chopped preserved lemon rind, chopped fresh herbs, scallions, and remaining 2 tablespoons of olive oil. Season with salt and pepper.

To serve, divide the lettuce leaves among each plate. Top each with 3 grilled sardines. Spoon the preserved lemon mixture on top. Garnish with a drizzle of olive oil, sprinkle with the flaked sea salt, and serve with lemon wedges.

CHEF'S NOTES: Ultrafresh sardines are fantastic cooked as is, but you can also brine them to add a little bit of sweet-and-salty flavor before cooking. Once the fish is brined, you can bake, broil, roast, or pan-sear as you like. The brining process can be done a day in advance. Follow the method on page 98.

A staple in Mediterranean Europe and Britain, sardines on toast has never quite taken hold here in North America. I'd like to change that. Sardines are an exceptional source of vitamin B12—essential to our brain health, nervous system, and the production of red blood cells—and vitamin D, which we need for healthy bones. For the most tender results, brine these pretty little fish for at least 30 minutes and up to 24 hours before cooking.

SIMPLE BRINE
1 cup white sugar
½ cup sea salt
4 cups water
1 Tbsp black peppercorns
2 bay leaves

TOMATO RELISH
1 lb tomatoes, seeded and chopped
½ red onion, thinly sliced
3 cloves garlic, finely chopped
½ cup extra-virgin olive oil
¼ cup red wine vinegar
⅓ cup chopped flat-leaf parsley
1 tsp sea salt
2 tsp coarsely ground black pepper

SARDINES
4 fresh sardines, anchovies, or herring, butterflied (see Notes)
2 Tbsp extra-virgin olive oil (divided), plus more for drizzling
4 thick slices artisan bread
½ lemon
Sea salt and coarsely ground black pepper
Chopped flat-leaf parsley, for garnish

SERVES 2 TO 4

SARDINES ON TOAST WITH TOMATO RELISH

SIMPLE BRINE Combine all the ingredients in a medium saucepan and bring to a boil over high heat. Cook for a few minutes or until the sugar has dissolved, set aside to cool, and then refrigerate until cold.

TOMATO RELISH Combine all the ingredients in a large nonreactive bowl. Taste and adjust seasoning with more salt and pepper if desired. Put ½ cup of the mixture into a blender and puree until smooth. Set both aside.

SARDINES Soak the sardines in the cold brine for 30 minutes or refrigerate in the brine for up to 24 hours.

When ready to serve, preheat the broiler and set the oven rack 4 inches below it. Remove the fish from the brine and pat dry with paper towels. Set the fish on a baking sheet and rub all over with 1 tablespoon of the olive oil. Set the baking sheet under the broiler and cook the fish for about 2 minutes or until the skin is browned. Turn the fish over and broil the other side for 2 to 3 more minutes or until the skin is browned and the flesh is opaque and flakes easily. Transfer to a plate.

Set the oven rack 6 inches below the broiler. Brush one side of each bread slice with the remaining tablespoon of olive oil and set on the baking sheet. Broil for 1 to 2 minutes or until golden brown.

To serve, spread each toast with tomato relish. Lay a sardine on top. Drizzle with the tomato relish puree, some additional olive oil, and a squeeze of lemon juice, and season with salt and pepper. Garnish with chopped parsley.

CHEF'S NOTES: You can ask your fishmonger to butterfly the sardines for you, but it's simple to do yourself. Use kitchen scissors or a sharp, thin knife to cut off the head, just behind the gills and front fin. You can cut off the tail or leave it on. Carefully, so as not to tear the delicate meat, cut or slice along the belly to open it up. Scrape out the innards. Turn the fish belly side down and gently press on the backbone, which will help loosen it from the flesh. Turn it over and carefully pull the backbone away from the flesh. If you've left the tail on, just snip it where the backbone meets the tail to free it. The sardines may be eaten simply brined or broiled.

½ cup Lime Vinaigrette
(page 147), plus extra
to serve
½ lb premium-quality
albacore tuna loin, cut
into ¼-inch-thick slices
(see Notes)
1 to 2 avocadoes, sliced
½ seedless English
cucumber, sliced
Flaked sea salt, to sprinkle

Albacore tuna served ice cold and raw is one of the great pleasures of living on the West Coast. The flesh shimmers with beautiful rosy iridescence, and the flavor is delicate and almost citrusy. I love to enhance that citrus note with a drizzle of lime vinaigrette, as in this easy crudo. While ceviche involves marinating with a lot of liquid, crudo is all about coating the fish with flavorful oils and just a touch of acidity and seasoning. Keep in mind, you should only eat fresh fish thawed from frozen and when you know it's premium quality.

ALBACORE TUNA CRUDO

Spoon about ½ cup of the lime vinaigrette onto a serving platter. Arrange the tuna slices, avocado, and cucumber segments on top. Sprinkle with sea salt. Spoon a few more tablespoons of lime vinaigrette over all. Serve immediately.

CHEF'S NOTES: Albacore is sold as frozen loins. If the loin looks a bit raggedy, trim the edges nice and neat (save the trimmings, poach them in a little olive oil, and use them in a sandwich or salad). If the loin has the belly meat attached (it's lighter in color and has more stripes of fat), slice it off and reserve it for a delicious tuna tartare.

Poke (pronounced po-kay) is a beloved mainstay of Hawaiian cuisine, with roots in Japanese chirashi (scattered sushi) bowls. Cubes of tender, sparkling-fresh fish are lightly dressed, usually with a little soy sauce and sesame oil, and then piled on bowls of fluffy steamed rice with a few other garnishes like avocado and seaweed. It's healthy, filling, fresh, and incredibly flavorful, especially with this miso-maple-lime vinaigrette. I use superfresh albacore here, but sashimi-grade wild salmon or yellowfin tuna also work well. If you don't like raw fish, try searing the fish briefly on all sides tataki style (page 103). Even cubed and barely cooked halibut would be a delicious alternative.

SERVES 6

TUNA POKE BOWL

MISO, MAPLE, AND LIME VINAIGRETTE In a small bowl, combine the lime zest and juice, mustard, miso, maple syrup, sambal oelek or Sriracha, if using, and salt. While whisking, slowly drizzle the oil in a thin steady stream until incorporated and the mixture is emulsified. Adjust seasoning to taste. (Alternatively, you can do this with an immersion blender or in a blender or small food processor.) Can be made ahead of time; will keep refrigerated for up to 2 weeks (although the lime flavor will start to weaken after a few days).

TUNA POKE Combine the quinoa and water or broth in a large saucepan. Bring to a boil over high heat, reduce to low, cover, and simmer for 15 minutes or until all the water is absorbed and quinoa is tender. Remove the pan from the heat and allow to stand, covered, for 10 minutes. Fluff with a fork. Allow to cool to a warm room temperature.

Steam the corn in a steamer insert set over a few inches of boiling water for about 5 minutes, or place in a microwave-safe dish with 2 tablespoons cold water and cook for 3 to 5 minutes. Allow to cool.

In a medium bowl, gently toss the diced tuna with just enough vinaigrette to coat.

To serve, divide the quinoa among 4 bowls. Top with the steamed corn, pineapple (or papaya), avocado, and tuna. Drizzle with more vinaigrette if desired. Sprinkle with the sesame seeds and nori. Serve with lime wedges.

MISO, MAPLE, AND LIME VINAIGRETTE
Zest and juice of ½ lime
1 tsp Dijon mustard
1½ tsp white miso paste
1½ tsp maple syrup
½ tsp sambal oelek or Sriracha (optional)
¼ tsp sea salt
½ cup canola oil

TUNA POKE
1½ cups quinoa (rinsed if instructed on the package)
3 cups water or broth
1½ cups fresh or frozen corn kernels
1 lb premium-quality albacore tuna loin, cut into ½-inch cubes (see Notes on page 100)
1½ cups chopped pineapple or papaya
1 large avocado, diced
¼ cup toasted sesame seeds, to sprinkle
1 sheet dried nori, sliced into thin strips, to sprinkle
1 lime, cut into wedges, for garnish

You've heard of seared ahi tuna steaks, right? Well that's essentially tataki. The flesh is flash-seared so it's crispy on the outside but still rare inside, resulting in a delicious contrast of textures and temperatures. Thinly sliced and arranged on a platter, it makes for an elegant first course, especially when topped with crunchy toasted sesame seeds and tahini vinaigrette. The rich, nutty flavor of the sesame seeds is a perfect match for the rare tuna.

SERVES 4

TUNA TATAKI

TAHINI, LEMON, AND HONEY VINAIGRETTE

½ cup extra-virgin olive oil
Zest and juice of 2 lemons
2 Tbsp honey
1½ Tbsp Dijon mustard
1 Tbsp tahini
1 tsp sea salt

TUNA

2 Tbsp canola oil
1½ lb albacore tuna loin
   (see Notes on page 100)
1 to 2 radishes, thinly sliced,
   for garnish
Radish sprouts, for garnish
Toasted sesame seeds, to
   sprinkle
Flaked sea salt, to sprinkle

TAHINI, LEMON, AND HONEY VINAIGRETTE
Combine all the ingredients in a medium bowl, whisking until well blended and emulsified. Taste and adjust seasoning with more lemon and salt if desired. Can be made ahead of time; will keep refrigerated for up to 2 weeks (although the lemon flavor will start to weaken after a few days).

TUNA Heat the oil in a large skillet set over medium-high heat until almost smoking. Add the tuna loin, and sear each side for 20 seconds or until golden but still rare to medium-rare on the inside.

Immediately transfer the tuna to a cutting board. Use a sharp knife to cut into ¼-inch-thick slices. Arrange the slices on a serving platter, garnish with the radishes and sprouts, and sprinkle with the sesame seeds and salt. Spoon over the vinaigrette and serve immediately.

ARTICHOKE PUREE
1 cup canned and drained
    artichoke hearts (not
    marinated)
1 Tbsp extra-virgin olive oil
Zest and juice of 1 lemon
Sea salt and coarsely
    ground black pepper

TUNA MELT
2 (5 oz) cans oil- or water-
    packed albacore tuna,
    drained
¼ cup mayonnaise
Sea salt and coarsely
    ground black pepper
4 large slices crusty bread
4 slices aged cheddar
½ cup grated white cheddar
1 to 2 tomatoes, thinly
    sliced

SERVES 2

BEST TUNA MELT EVER

ARTICHOKE PUREE Puree the artichoke hearts in a blender or small food processor or with an immersion blender until smooth. Stir in the olive oil and lemon zest and juice. Season with salt and pepper to taste.

TUNA MELT Preheat the oven to 350°F. Have ready baking sheets, lining one with parchment paper.

Combine the tuna and mayonnaise in a bowl and mix well. Season with salt and pepper to taste.

Spread the artichoke puree on each slice of bread, top with the tuna mixture and a slice of cheddar, and arrange on the baking sheet (without parchment). Spread the grated cheddar on the parchment-lined baking sheet into 4 sections to make cheese crisps. Bake for 7 to 10 minutes or until the bread is toasted around the edges, the cheese slices have melted, and the crisps are golden and crispy. Remove from the oven, add a few slices of tomato, and season with salt and pepper. Serve open-faced with a cheese crisp.

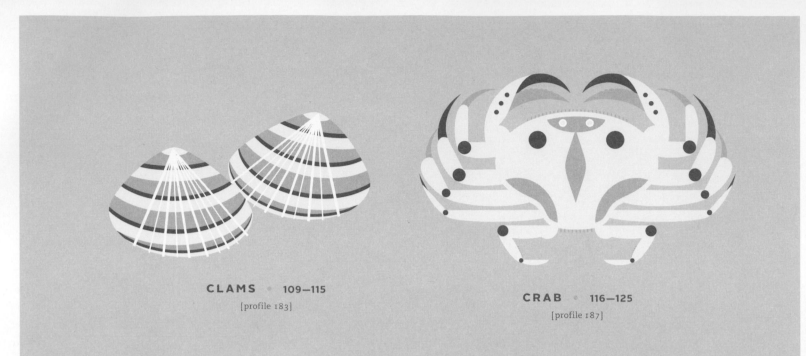

CLAMS • 109—115

[profile 183]

CRAB • 116—125

[profile 187]

SHELLFISH

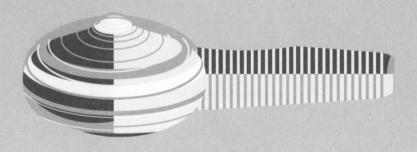

GEODUCK • 126—127

[profile 189]

MUSSELS • 128—135

[profile 195]

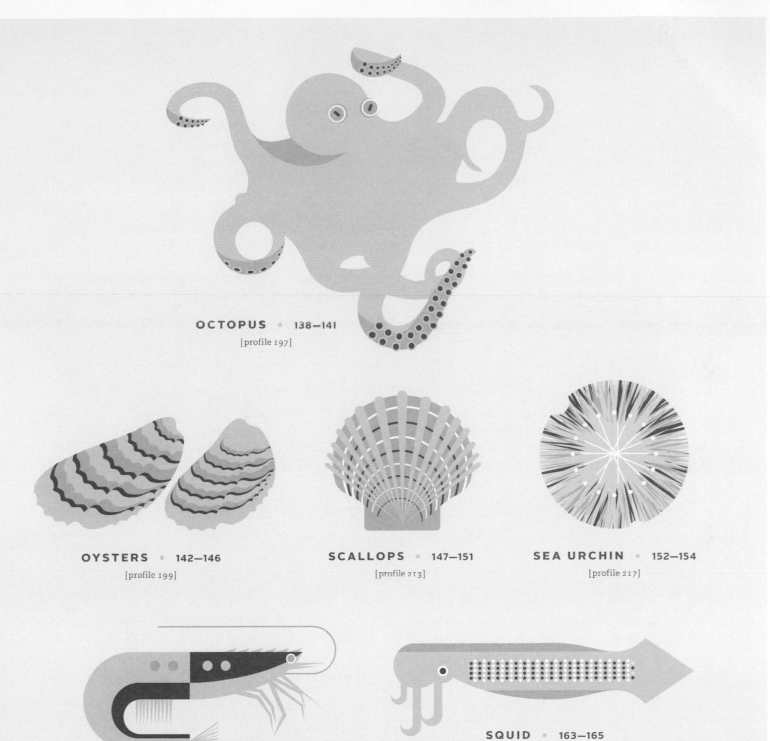

OCTOPUS • 138—141

[profile 197]

OYSTERS • 142—146

[profile 199]

SCALLOPS • 147—151

[profile 213]

SEA URCHIN • 152—154

[profile 217]

SHRIMP • 155—162

[profile 219]

SQUID • 163—165

[profile 223]

SHELLFISH

WHEN I COME into my kitchen with the first live spot prawns of the season, everybody working in the restaurant, front and back of house, stops what they're doing. They'll pluck the biggest ones they can get their hands on, live and leaping, from the crate, peel back their papery pink skins, and pop the sweet, plump flesh into their mouths. There's such a buzz around these feisty creatures. Shellfish are exciting!

Clams, mussels, and oysters are beautiful raw, steamed, or baked; squid and octopus love the grill; and my favorite way to cook crab and lobster is in a big pot of seawater. Always hang onto the shells—they make a beautiful seafood broth when boiled with onions, garlic, and aromatic herbs. You could throw in fish bones too.

I encourage you to try the Coastal Dungeness Crab Boil (page 125) if you're entertaining—it's the most enjoyable way I can think of to feed your friends. And if you're feeling adventurous, why not whip up some sea urchin custards (page 152)? Tell people what they're eating, and then sit back and witness the power of this instant icebreaker.

I first had butter clams raw at a shellfish tasting, right on Fisherman's Wharf in San Francisco. I was with the Northern Chefs Alliance, a think tank of American and Canadian chefs committed to cleaning up our food systems and getting adventurous with regional specialties. The butter clam is one of the few Pacific clams that's tender enough to eat raw. Simply served with a squeeze of zingy lemon, the true flavor of this shellfish shines through. A dollop of kimchi aioli takes them from elemental to decadent.

SERVES 4

KIMCHI AIOLI
1 egg
1 egg yolk
Zest and juice of 2 limes
1½ Tbsp Dijon mustard
½ tsp Sriracha
½ tsp sea salt
1 cup canola oil
2 Tbsp finely chopped
  kimchi

BUTTER CLAMS
2 lb live butter clams
Crushed ice or rock salt
1 lemon or lime, halved

RAW BUTTER CLAMS WITH KIMCHI AIOLI

KIMCHI AIOLI In a food processor or blender (or use an immersion blender), combine the egg, egg yolk, lime zest and juice, mustard, Sriracha, and salt. With the machine running, slowly add the oil in a thin steady stream. When the mixture is emulsified and thickened and all the oil has been incorporated, stir in the kimchi. Taste and adjust seasoning with more salt or lime if desired. Can be made ahead of time; will keep refrigerated for up to 3 days.

BUTTER CLAMS Rinse the clams under cold water for at least 5 minutes, and discard any that are open and won't close when tapped or that have broken shells. Scrub off any debris.

Pour a ½-inch deep layer of crushed ice or rock salt on a serving platter. Shuck the clams, reserving them on their half shell. Nestle the shells into the ice or salt. Top each with a squeeze of lemon or lime juice. Serve with kimchi aioli on the side.

CHEF'S NOTES: The clams may be substituted with razor clams or thinly sliced geoduck.

I'll often serve this showstopper as an appetizer—wait till you see your guests' eyes widen when the steaming baked-potato-and-clam double-stuffed shells are set down before them on the table. Every forkful of this dish-in-a-shell brings together the ocean brininess of the clams with the soothing buttery sweetness of a golden potato crust. Spectacular!

MASHED POTATO
½ lb Yukon gold potatoes, peeled and cut into 1-inch pieces
2 Tbsp unsalted butter
¼ cup whole milk
2 tsp whole grain mustard
2 tsp prepared horseradish
1 scallion, chopped
Smoked sea salt (see Notes on page 146) and coarsely ground black pepper

CLAMS
1½ lb live butter clams
1 Tbsp unsalted butter
1 shallot, finely chopped
¼ cup white wine
Smoked sea salt, for garnish (see Notes on page 146)
Zest of ½ lemon, for garnish
Extra-virgin olive oil, to drizzle
Crostini, to serve

BUTTER CLAMS STUFFED WITH GOLDEN POTATO, HORSERADISH, AND LEMON

MASHED POTATO Fill a saucepan with 2 inches of water and bring to a boil over high heat. Set a steamer insert in the pot and add the diced potatoes. Cover and steam for 20 minutes, or until completely tender.

Discard the water in the saucepan and remove the steamer insert. Off the heat, add the steamed potatoes, butter, milk, mustard, horseradish, and scallions back to the saucepan. Mash until smooth. Season with salt and pepper to taste.

CLAMS Rinse the clams under cold water for at least 5 minutes, and discard any that are open and won't close when tapped or that have broken shells. Scrub off any debris.

Preheat the oven to 375°F. Melt the butter in a large pot over medium heat, add the shallots, and sauté for 1 minute. Add the clams and wine, cover, and steam for 5 to 7 minutes or until clams are just open. Remove the pot from the heat and discard any unopened clams.

Pop the top shell off and discard. Reserve the bottom shell and release the clam from the shell. Top each clam with 2 to 3 tablespoons of mashed potato, place on a baking sheet, and bake for 20 minutes or until golden brown.

Garnish with the smoked salt and lemon zest, and then drizzle over a little olive oil. Serve warm with crostini.

Clams steamed in beer is a classic dish. But when cooking with beer, it's a good idea to reach for something on the lighter end of the spectrum. Beer with a strong hop profile, like a West Coast IPA, can add too much bitterness. In this case I'd go with a pale ale such as Fat Tug from Driftwood Brewery (Victoria, BC), with its beautiful black pepper flavors, or Vaporizer by Double Mountain Brewery (Portland, Oregon), with its dry and lemony finish.

SERVES 4

STEAMED CLAMS WITH PALE ALE, LEEKS, AND BUTTER

4 lb live clams such as littleneck, Manila, or savory (purple varnish)
1 Tbsp olive oil
2 shallots, thinly sliced
1 tsp sea salt
2 tsp coarsely ground black pepper
5 cloves garlic, crushed
1 small leek, white and light green parts, halved and thinly sliced into half moons
2 cups pale ale
2 Tbsp unsalted butter
Artisan bread, to serve

Rinse the clams under cold water for at least 5 minutes, and discard any that are open and won't close when tapped or that have broken shells. Scrub off any debris.

Heat the olive oil in a large, heavy-bottomed pot over medium heat. Add the shallots, season with salt and pepper, and sauté for 3 to 5 minutes or until shallots are tender and translucent. Add the garlic and leeks, and sauté for 1 minute more. Add the clams and beer, cover, and cook for 5 minutes or until the clams open up. Discard any that haven't opened. Add the butter and stir until melted.

Transfer the clams and broth into a family-style bowl or divide among single-serving bowls. Serve with bread on the side.

The beauty of this dish lies in its simplicity. Garlic, shallots, and a little white wine form the base, and the clams contribute their own juice during cooking. The resulting light and flavorful sauce perfectly coats twirls of pasta for a comforting one-pot dish.

SERVES 4

3 lb live clams such as littleneck, Manila, or savory (purple varnish)
1 lb dried spaghetti
½ cup extra-virgin olive oil
3 Tbsp unsalted butter
1 shallot, finely chopped
5 cloves garlic, thinly sliced
1 tsp chili flakes
¼ cup clam juice
¼ cup dry white wine
3 Tbsp finely chopped flat-leaf parsley
Zest and juice of 2 lemons
Sea salt and coarsely ground black pepper, to taste
Warm crusty bread, to serve

SPAGHETTI WITH CLAMS, CHILI, AND OLIVE OIL

Rinse the clams under cold water for at least 5 minutes, and discard any that are open and won't close when tapped or that have broken shells. Scrub off any debris.

Bring a large pot of water to a boil over high heat and salt generously. Add the pasta and cook until al dente, according to manufacturer's instructions. Drain the pasta.

Meanwhile, heat the olive oil and butter in a large shallow sauté pan over medium heat. Add the shallots and sauté for 5 minutes or until tender. Add the garlic and chili flakes and sauté for another minute. Add the clams and cook for 1 minute. Pour in the clam juice and wine, cover, and allow clams to steam for 2 to 3 minutes or until opened. Discard any that haven't opened.

Stir in the cooked, drained pasta, parsley, and lemon zest and juice. Season with salt and pepper, to taste. Divide among bowls and serve immediately with buttered slices of warm bread.

What makes this Mediterranean-inspired clam chowder so speedy is the Walter Caesar Mix, one of the most-used shortcut ingredients in my chef's arsenal. Sure, it's meant to be a cocktail mixer, but it's far more versatile than that. I've used it in bouillabaisse, paella, soups, and stews. I like that it's made in small batches with natural ingredients and clam juice from sustainably harvested clams.

SERVES 4

3 lb live clams such as littleneck, Manila, or savory (purple varnish), rinsed
2 cups white wine
2 Tbsp unsalted butter
2 Tbsp olive oil
1 red onion, chopped
2 stalks celery, diced
1 small bulb fennel, diced
2 cloves garlic, chopped
1 tsp sea salt
1 tsp coarsely ground black pepper
8 cups Walter Caesar Mix (see Notes)
3 large Yukon gold potatoes, cut into ½-inch cubes
1 cup fresh or frozen corn kernels
1 geoduck body meat (page 126), chopped (optional)
3 Tbsp chopped scallions, for garnish
1 Tbsp extra-virgin olive oil, to drizzle
Kelp and Smoked Sea Salt Scones (page 172), to serve (optional)

CLAM AND TOMATO CHOWDER

If using live clams, rinse the clams under cold water for at least 5 minutes, and discard any that are open and won't close when tapped or that have broken shells. Scrub off any debris.

Place the clams in a medium saucepan and add the wine. Cover and bring to a simmer over medium-high heat. Cook until clams open, about 10 minutes. Remove the pan from the heat, and discard any clams that aren't open. Set aside to cool. Strain the cooking liquid through a fine-mesh sieve or cheesecloth to remove any grit, and reserve the clam broth. Roughly chop the clams.

In a large saucepan, heat the butter and olive oil over medium heat. Add the onions, celery, and fennel, and sauté for 7 minutes or until onions are translucent. Stir in the garlic and salt and pepper, and sauté for another minute until fragrant.

Pour in the reserved clam broth, stirring to scrape up any browned bits, and cook for 3 to 4 minutes or until the liquid is reduced by half. Add the Caesar mix and bring to a boil over high heat. Reduce the heat to medium-low and simmer for 20 minutes.

Add the potatoes and cook for another 10 minutes or until cooked through. Add the clams, corn, and geoduck body meat, if using. Simmer until warmed through for another 5 minutes. Taste and adjust seasoning with more salt and pepper if desired.

Ladle into individual bowls, garnish with scallions, and drizzle with extra-virgin olive oil. Serve with kelp scones, if desired.

CHEF'S NOTES: If you can't get Walter Caesar Mix, combine 6 cups tomato juice and 2 cups clam juice with about 2 tablespoons horseradish and lemon juice to taste.

Snow crab thrives in colder waters—it's not as sweet as Dungeness nor as sexy as the beastly king crab, but it has its own distinctive delicate and briny qualities that make it special. As with any crab cake, less is more—it should barely hold together when you sink your teeth in. Most recipes use breadcrumbs for coating, but I prefer cornmeal for a most satisfyingly crispy crunch.

STEAMED CRAB
3 (2 to 3 lb) live snow crabs

CORN RELISH
2 cups fresh corn kernels, boiled
2 scallions, chopped
1 Tbsp extra-virgin olive oil
1 lemon or lime
Sea salt and coarsely ground black pepper

SMOKED CHILI MAYO
1 egg
1 egg yolk
2 tsp Dijon mustard
Juice of 1 lemon
½ tsp sea salt
½ tsp coarsely ground black pepper
1 cup canola oil
1 Tbsp chopped canned chipotle pepper

SERVES 6
(MAKES 12 CRAB CAKES)

SNOW CRAB CAKES WITH SMOKED CHILI MAYO, SWEET AND SOUR PEPPERS, AND CORN RELISH

STEAMED CRAB Chill the live crabs in the freezer for 15 minutes before cooking—it slows them down and makes them easier to get into the water. Set a steamer insert over a few inches of water in a large stockpot. Once the water comes to a boil, place the crabs onto the steamer basket, cover the pot, and cook for 12 minutes. Remove crabs with tongs and plunge in ice-cold water until cool enough to handle.

To clean the crabs, pull off the shell from the back. Reserve any liquid, which you can use to make crab stock. Discard the pale-greenish innards (tomalley) inside the shell, picking off larger pieces with your fingers, and running fresh cold water over what's left. Pull off the gills, which look like pods that are barely attached at the sides of the crab. Use your hands to break off the mouth parts. Turn the crab over and pull off the triangular "apron." Crack open harder shells with pliers or heavy-duty shellfish crackers—avoid mallets as they break up the meat. With kitchen shears, snip open the legs so you can gently pull or pick out the flesh.

CORN RELISH Combine the corn, scallions, and olive oil in a bowl. Add a squeeze of lemon (or lime) and season with salt and pepper.

SMOKED CHILI MAYO In a food processor or blender (or using an immersion blender), combine the egg, egg yolk, mustard, lemon juice, and salt and pepper. With the machine running, slowly add the oil in a thin steady stream. When the mixture is emulsified and thickened and all the oil has been incorporated, add the chipotles to taste. (Proceed with caution—you only want a hint of smokiness and spiciness as the crab is delicate.) Taste and adjust seasoning with more salt, pepper, or lemon if desired. Can be made ahead of time; will keep refrigerated for up to 3 days.

SWEET AND SOUR PEPPERS Preheat the oven to 400°F. Line a baking sheet with aluminum foil, put the peppers on the sheet, and roast for 10 to 12 minutes. Turn them over and roast for another 10 to 12 minutes, or until the skin is charred and soft. Set aside until cool enough to handle. Peel off the skins, slice peppers open to remove the seeds, and slice into ¼-inch-wide strips.

Transfer the peppers to a bowl, and add the olive oil, vinegar, and honey.

CRAB CAKES In a large bowl, lightly mix together the crab, ½ cup of the mayo, corn, chives, and lemon zest and juice. Add a little more mayo if needed to allow the mixture to just barely hold together. (For the best texture, don't use too much mayo or break up the crab too much.)

Put the cornmeal in a shallow bowl. Use a ⅓-cup measure to scoop the crab mixture and shape it into a thick patty. Dip the patty in the cornmeal and set on a baking sheet. Repeat with the remaining mixture.

Heat some of the oil in a heavy-bottomed cast-iron or stainless-steel skillet over medium-high heat. In batches, cook the patties for about 3 minutes or until golden brown. Turn over and cook for another 3 minutes. Transfer to a paper-towel-lined plate to drain.

To serve, spoon the corn relish and sweet-and-sour peppers on each plate. Place 2 crab cakes on top and spoon smoked chili mayo over them. Garnish with watercress leaves and diced avocado.

CHEF'S NOTES: Keep the crab shells and body for crab stock.

SWEET AND SOUR PEPPERS
1 yellow bell pepper
1 red bell pepper
1 Tbsp extra-virgin olive oil
1 Tbsp red wine vinegar
1 tsp honey

CRAB CAKES
4 cups snow crabmeat, from about 3 (2 to 3 lb) live snow crabs (see page 116)
About ¾ cup Smoked Chili Mayo (see page 116), plus extra to serve
1 cup fresh corn kernels
2 to 3 Tbsp chopped fresh chives
Zest and juice of 1 lemon
1 to 2 cups cornmeal, for dredging
¼ cup canola oil, for frying
6 stems watercress, for garnish
1 avocado, diced, for garnish

Quick, simple, and bursting with flavor, these mini crab tacos are real crowd-pleasers. They can go from game-day snack to cocktail party nibble with ease. The light and crispy shells are made with deep-fried wonton wrappers, which perfectly showcase the tender flesh of Dungeness crab. The average crab yields about half a pound of meat (about 1½ cups), so you'll just need one crab for this dish. It's far cheaper to cook and pick your own crab. But if time is of the essence, and your budget doesn't allow for already picked crabmeat, try substituting shrimp, wild salmon, albacore, lingcod, or really any fish you like.

MAKES 12

MINI DUNGENESS CRAB TACOS

TACO SHELLS Heat several inches of oil in a medium heavy-bottomed saucepan, Dutch oven, or deep-fryer to 340°F. Place a wrapper in a taco shell maker and gently lower it into the oil. Cook for 30 seconds or until golden. Transfer to a plate lined with paper towels. (Alternatively, shape a piece of aluminum foil into a thick rectangle and drape the wrapper over it. Use tongs to hold the wrapper onto the foil as you lower it into the oil. Continue holding it in place until it's done.)

TACOS To steam the crab and extract the meat from the legs and main shell, follow the instructions on page 116.

Cut each avocado in half lengthwise and remove the pit. Scoop the flesh into a medium bowl. Using a fork, coarsely mash the avocado with the lemon juice and olive oil. Season with salt and pepper to taste. Put spoonfuls onto serving plates.

Stuff about 2 tablespoons of the crabmeat into each taco shell, and set them into the mashed avocado, which will help hold them upright. Top with a little vinaigrette and garnish with the radishes and radish sprouts. Add dots of vinaigrette around the plate. Sprinkle with a pinch of Shichimi Togarashi. Serve the tacos with lime wedges on the side, and instruct guests to scoop up a little of the avocado with every taco.

CHEF'S NOTES: Shichimi Togarashi is a popular Japanese spice blend and table condiment that is made of coarse ground red chili, sansho (a type of Japanese pepper), roasted orange peel, black and white sesame seeds, hemp seed, ground ginger, and nori. It is available at Asian markets.

TACO SHELLS
Canola oil, for deep-frying
12 round gyoza or wonton wrappers

TACOS
½ lb (about 1½ cups) crabmeat, from 1 (2 to 3 lb) Dungeness or snow crab
1 ripe avocado
Juice of ½ lemon
2 tsp olive oil
Sea salt and coarsely ground black pepper
About ¼ cup Miso, Maple, and Lime Vinaigrette (page 101)
3 radishes, thinly sliced, for garnish
¾ cup radish sprouts, for garnish
Shichimi Togarashi, to sprinkle (see Notes)
Lime wedges, to serve

SERVES 4

GREEN GODDESS DRESSING
1 ripe avocado
Zest and juice of 1 lime
Zest and juice of ½ lemon
1 Tbsp white wine vinegar
¼ cup extra-virgin olive oil
¼ cup canola oil
½ cup water
½ tsp sea salt
½ tsp coarsely ground black pepper
¼ cup chopped fresh chives
1 Tbsp fresh tarragon

SALAD
1 lb king crabmeat (about 4 lb crab legs)
2 red, yellow, or orange bell peppers
1 lb green beans, ends trimmed
4 eggs
2 to 3 small heads butter lettuce, leaves torn
2 cups assorted cherry tomatoes, halved
1 avocado, pitted, peeled, and sliced
1 cup fresh whole-milk ricotta or fromage frais
Warm crusty bread, to serve

KING CRAB COBB SALAD

GREEN GODDESS DRESSING Halve the avocado lengthwise, remove the pit, and scoop the flesh into a blender or food processor. Add the remaining ingredients and blend or process until smooth. Taste and adjust seasoning with more citrus juice, salt, or pepper if desired.

SALAD Fill a large stockpot with a few inches of water and bring to a boil. Place the crab legs in a steamer insert, set in the pot and steam, covered, for 5 minutes. Remove the crab, and use kitchen shears to cut the shells lengthwise to make it easier to remove the meat. Refrigerate until later use.

Preheat the oven to 400°F. Line a baking sheet with aluminum foil, put the peppers on the sheet, and roast for 10 to 12 minutes. Turn them over and roast for another 10 to 12 minutes, or until the skin is charred and soft. Set aside until cool enough to handle. Peel off the skins, slice peppers open to remove the seeds, and chop.

Bring a large pot of salted water to a boil. Set a large bowl of ice-cold water nearby. Add the green beans to the boiling water and blanch for 3 minutes. Use tongs or a slotted spoon to transfer the green beans immediately to the ice water to stop the cooking. When cool, drain and cut lengthwise.

Set a steamer insert over the pot of boiling water (or if you only have collapsible inserts, drain off all but a few inches of the hot water and set the insert inside). Set the eggs in the steamer, cover, and steam for 10 minutes. Remove and plunge in cold water to stop the cooking. When cool, peel the eggs and slice, or quarter into wedges.

Arrange the lettuce leaves on a serving platter or divide among 4 individual bowls. Arrange the peppers, green beans, eggs, cherry tomatoes, sliced avocado, and crabmeat (½ cup per person) on top. Dot with the ricotta (or fromage frais) and pour the dressing over the top. Serve with warm crusty bread.

Mac 'n' cheese is already one of the most indulgent comfort foods ever created. But when you add sweet Dungeness crabmeat, it becomes downright deluxe. Of course, carbs swaddled in cheese aren't exactly a nutritionist's dream, so I have a trick for adding a little bit of virtue to this soul-satisfying dish: pureed cauliflower. This crucifer adds a wallop of vitamins, minerals, and cancer-fighting compounds—and it helps thicken the sauce, too.

2 (2 to 3 lb) Dungeness crabs, for 3 cups crabmeat (or cooked sidestripe or pink shrimp)

1 lb dried macaroni

1 Tbsp canola oil

1 onion, finely chopped

1 clove garlic, finely chopped

1 small head cauliflower, stem removed, florets chopped

4 cups whole milk

½ cup mascarpone

1 Tbsp Dijon mustard

2 cups grated sharp white cheddar

1 cup finely grated Parmesan

Zest and juice of 1 lemon

2 Tbsp chopped fresh chives, plus extra for garnish

Sea salt and coarsely ground black pepper

SERVES 6

DUNGENESS CRAB AND WHITE CHEDDAR MAC 'N' CHEESE

To steam the crab and extract the meat from the legs and main shell, follow the instructions on page 116.

Bring a large pot of water to a boil over high heat, and salt generously. Add the pasta and cook until al dente, according to the manufacturer's instructions. Drain the pasta.

Heat the oil in a large pot over medium heat, add the onions, and sauté for 7 minutes or until translucent. Stir in the garlic and cook for another 30 seconds or until fragrant. Add the cauliflower and milk, bring to a simmer, and cook for 20 minutes.

Strain the milk using a colander or strainer over a bowl. Transfer the solids to a blender and puree until smooth.

Return the strained milk to the saucepan and set over low heat. Add the mascarpone and mustard, and cook for 3 to 5 minutes. Stir in the cheddar and Parmesan, whisking until melted (but do not allow it to boil).

Stir half the pureed vegetables into the mixture, then add as much as needed to create a thick sauce. Stir in the crab, lemon zest and juice, and chives. Season with salt and pepper to taste.

Add the cooked pasta, stir until warmed through, and serve garnished with more chives.

CHEF'S NOTES: This makes a great baked pasta dish. Transfer the contents to a greased 4-quart baking dish, sprinkle with ½ cup grated cheddar or breadcrumbs, and bake in an oven preheated to 350°F for 30 to 40 minutes or until the top is golden and sauce is bubbly.

The vanilla in this coconut-rich sauce is a secret weapon to temper the fire of the ginger, without making the sauce cloyingly sweet. Eating the curry-drenched crab legs is a messy endeavor, but that's half the fun. Serve this dish as part of an Asian-inspired feast, or double the ingredients if you want to tuck into it as a stand-alone family meal.

SERVES 2 TO 4

1 (2 to 3 lb) Dungeness crab
2 cups coconut milk
1 cup Vegetable Stock
   (page 138), Fish Stock
   (page 90), or chicken
   stock
1 (2-inch) piece fresh ginger,
   peeled and sliced
1 Tbsp chopped garlic
2 scallions, chopped
2 Tbsp Thai or Indian curry
   paste
1 vanilla bean
Sea salt and coarsely
   ground black pepper
2 yellow potatoes, peeled
   and cut into ¾-inch
   cubes
½ cup sliced hearts of palm
   (see Notes)
½ cup torn oyster
   mushrooms
¼ cup fresh or frozen peas
¼ cup sliced sugar snap
   peas
2 cups steamed rice,
   to serve
Lemon wedges or Lime
   Pickle (page 147),
   to serve

CRAB CURRY WITH GINGER

To steam the crab, follow the instructions on page 116, and then cut the crab through the body into eighths (instead of extracting the crabmeat).

Combine the coconut milk, stock, ginger, garlic, scallions, and curry paste in a large pot. Split the vanilla bean in half lengthwise, scrape out the seeds with the back of a knife, and add to the pot along with the pod. Cover and bring to a simmer over medium-high heat. Season with salt and pepper and add the potatoes. Cover and bring back to a simmer, reduce to medium-low, and cook for about 25 minutes or until potatoes are tender. Remove the vanilla bean pod and discard.

Add the crab pieces, hearts of palm, mushrooms, peas, and snap peas. Cook until warmed through. Divide steamed rice among bowls and ladle the crab and curry sauce over the top. Garnish with lemon wedges or lime pickle. Serve with mallets, crab picks, and bowls for the shells.

CHEF'S NOTES: I prefer fresh hearts of palm, which you can find at Asian markets. If you can't find them, just used canned.

A boil-up of tender Dungeness crab legs, baby potatoes, and juicy corn on the cob is the ultimate shared dining experience—especially if you're cooking it in a great big pot of seawater over a beach campfire. What sets this one apart is the savory-sweet stone-fruit butter that gets tossed in right before serving. This butter is delicious on just about any barbecued seafood, or even grilled tofu or seasonal vegetables, giving each bite the sweet taste of summer.

COASTAL DUNGENESS CRAB BOIL

STONE FRUIT BUTTER Combine all the ingredients in a bowl or food processor and mix or process until well blended. Scrape the butter onto a piece of plastic wrap, and then shape and roll it into a 2-inch-thick log. Refrigerate until needed. (Can be stored up to 5 days in the refrigerator or 6 months in the freezer.)

CRAB BOIL Bring a large stockpot of water to a boil over high heat. Salt generously (it should taste like seawater). Carefully place the crabs head first into the boiling water. When the water returns to a boil, cook for 15 minutes (or 20 minutes for 3-pound crabs). Remove crabs with tongs and plunge in ice-cold water until cool enough to handle. Keep the pot of water warm.

To clean the crabs, pull off the shell from the back. Discard any liquid (you can scoop out and save the golden "crab butter" to serve with the crab). Pull off the gills, which look like pods that are barely attached at the sides of the crab. Use your hands to break off the mouth parts. Turn the crab over and pull off the triangular "apron."

Bring the water back to a boil and add the potatoes. Boil until tender, about 15 minutes. Use a slotted spoon to transfer to a platter and tent with aluminum foil to keep warm.

Add the corn and cook until tender, about 5 minutes. Transfer to the platter with the potatoes.

Return the crab to the water just to heat through, about 3 minutes. Drain and cut each crab into quarters. Return the corn and potatoes to the empty (but still warm) pot, add the peach (or apricot or plum) slices and stone fruit butter. Toss the pot or gently stir, allowing the butter to melt and coat everything.

Arrange the crab, corn, and potatoes on the serving platter. Add some more dollops of butter. Provide mallets, crab picks, and bowls for the shells. Serve with crusty bread or kelp scones, green beans, and your favorite ice-cold craft beer.

CHEF'S NOTES: To roast garlic, slice the top third off of a head of garlic to expose the cloves. Drizzle with olive oil, wrap in aluminum foil, and roast at 400°F for 30 to 40 minutes or until soft. Or if you have any leftover garlic confit from the mussel stew on page 135 or the garganelli with shrimp on page 161, use a couple cloves from that.

Chill the live crabs in the freezer for 15 minutes before cooking—it slows them down and makes them easier to get into the water.

STONE FRUIT BUTTER
½ cup chopped fresh stone fruit such as peaches, apricots, or plums
1 cup (2 sticks) unsalted butter, softened
1 Tbsp honey or maple syrup
1 Tbsp white balsamic vinegar
1 Tbsp roasted garlic (see Notes)
1½ tsp smoked paprika
Zest and juice of ½ lime or lemon
1 tsp sea salt

CRAB BOIL
Sea salt
2 (2 to 3 lb) live Dungeness crabs (see Notes)
2 lb baby yellow or red potatoes, unpeeled
6 ears of fresh corn, halved crosswise
½ peach, apricot, or plum, sliced
¼ cup Stone Fruit Butter (see above)
Crusty bread or Kelp and Smoked Sea Salt Scones (page 172), to serve
Steamed green beans, to serve

Geoduck clams are somewhat blush-inducing with their long and wrinkly form. The fatty body meat and the long tube (siphon) that protrudes from the shell have distinctive tastes and textures—both worth exploring. This recipe is all about the tube, which is like octopus or calamari in texture but with a little crunch. Served sliced on crispy baked-wonton nachos, along with avocado and a piquant grapefruit vinaigrette, geoduck makes for an exciting appetizer.

SERVES 6

GRAPEFRUIT VINAIGRETTE
Zest and juice of
½ grapefruit
2 tsp Dijon mustard
½ tsp sea salt
½ cup canola oil

GEODUCK NACHOS
24 round gyoza or wonton
wrappers (about one
10 oz package; see Notes)
1 (1½ lb) live geoduck
2 ripe avocados
2 Tbsp lemon juice (about
1 lemon)
1 Tbsp extra-virgin olive oil
Sea salt and coarsely ground
black pepper
1 ruby red grapefruit,
segmented
Lime zest, for garnish
2 scallions, chopped, for
garnish

GEODUCK NACHOS WITH AVOCADO AND GRAPEFRUIT VINAIGRETTE

GRAPEFRUIT VINAIGRETTE Combine the grapefruit zest and juice, mustard, and salt in a small bowl. While whisking, slowly drizzle the oil in a thin steady stream until incorporated and the mixture is emulsified. Adjust seasoning to taste. (Alternatively, you can do this with an immersion blender or in a blender or small food processor.) Can be made ahead of time; will keep refrigerated for up to 2 weeks (although the grapefruit flavor will start to weaken after a few days).

GEODUCK NACHOS Preheat the oven to 325°F. Line 2 baking sheets with parchment paper. Spread the wonton skins on the baking sheets, and bake for 15 minutes or until golden brown. Set aside to cool.

Meanwhile, to prepare the geoduck, bring a large pot of water to a boil. Place a bowl of ice water nearby. The clam's shell will be slightly open. Slice between the shell and the meat on both sides to separate the adductor muscle from the shell and allow it to open. Open the shell, pull out the meat, and cut off the siphon tube. Reserve the body meat for another use (it's delicious finely diced and sautéed in butter for just a few seconds or added to the Clam and Tomato Chowder on page 114), but discard the sack hanging from it. Add the tube to the boiling water and

cook for 1 to 2 minutes. Transfer the tube to a bowl of ice-cold water to stop the cooking. Peel off the skin. Halve the tube lengthwise and thinly slice.

Cut the avocados in half lengthwise and remove the pit. Scoop the flesh into a medium bowl. Using a fork, coarsely mash the avocado with the lemon juice and olive oil. Season with salt and pepper to taste.

When ready to serve, slice the grapefruit segments crosswise into thirds. Spoon a little of the avocado mixture into each wonton crisp, add 2 slices of geoduck, and then drizzle with the vinaigrette. Garnish with lime zest and scallions.

CHEF'S NOTES: Wonton wrappers come square or round, and some are thinner than others, so a 10-ounce package might have 30 or it might have 50. It all depends on the brand. They also go by many different names— wonton skins, gyoza wrappers, pot sticker skins, you get the idea. For this recipe, just about any brand will do, although I prefer round shapes. If you can only find square, cut them in half diagonally to make triangles. Bake up any leftovers to serve with soup, chowder, or the marinated mussel salad on page 129.

This dish is loosely inspired by a dish created by Barton Seaver—chef, author, and champion of sustainability—when he was a guest chef for a Global Aquaculture Alliance event in Vancouver (I recommend you check out his TED Talk, "Sustainable Seafood? Let's Get Smart"). The plump chilled mussels and meaty green olives are bathed in a sweet-savory mix of orange and smoked paprika. They're a fantastic appetizer on wonton crisps or sourdough toasts to serve alongside a dry Manzanilla sherry.

SERVES 4

MUSSEL SALAD WITH ORANGES, OLIVES, AND SMOKED PAPRIKA

2 lb live mussels
1 Tbsp canola oil
1 shallot, chopped
Juice of 4 oranges (1 cup, divided)
2 oranges, segmented
½ cup pitted and quartered green olives such as Castelvetrano
2 to 3 Tbsp extra-virgin olive oil
1 tsp smoked paprika
1 tsp sea salt
Zest and juice of 1 lemon
1 garlic clove, very thinly sliced
Toasted baguette slices or baked wonton chips (page 126), to serve

Rinse the mussels under cold water, and discard any that are open and won't close when tapped or that have broken shells. Scrub off any debris and pull off the beard.

Heat the canola oil in a large pot over medium heat. Add the shallots, and sauté for 5 minutes or until softened and translucent. Add ½ cup of the orange juice and bring to a boil. Add the mussels, cover, and cook for about 2 minutes. (Do not overcook. Mussels cook very quickly. You know they're ready when the shells are open.) Use a slotted spoon to transfer the mussels to a baking sheet and allow to cool. Discard any that are unopened. (Reserve the mussel liquid to use in a chowder or when you need a shellfish stock.)

Remove the mussels from their shells and place in a bowl. Add the remaining ½ cup orange juice, orange segments, olives, olive oil, paprika, and salt. Stir to combine. Stir in the lemon zest and juice and garlic slices.

Serve the mussel salad in a shallow bowl with toasted baguette slices or wonton chips.

This is the dish that made my middle son, Max, a mussels convert. At eight years old, he was willing to try interesting-looking ingredients, but needed them to taste somewhat familiar. Apples of course are approachable for kids, as are melted butter and soy sauce—which is what tamari is, with the added bonus of usually being gluten free. You can typically convince children to try any seafood if you make it sweet, salty, and rich all at once.

3 lb live mussels
1 Tbsp canola oil
1 shallot, roughly chopped
1 Granny Smith apple, peeled, cored, and roughly chopped
2 Tbsp tamari
2 cups apple juice
2 Tbsp unsalted butter
Juice of 1 lemon
Crusty artisan bread, to serve

SERVES 4

STEAMED MUSSELS WITH APPLES AND TAMARI BUTTER

Rinse the mussels under cold water, and discard any that are open and won't close when tapped or that have broken shells. Scrub off any debris and pull off the beard.

Heat the oil in a large pot over medium heat, add the shallots and apples, and sauté for 5 minutes or until shallots are tender and translucent. Add the tamari and apple juice and bring to a boil. Add the mussels, cover, and cook for 2 minutes or until the shells just open up. (Do not overcook. Mussels cook very quickly. You know they're ready when the shells are open.) Discard any that don't open. Add the butter and lemon juice, stirring until the butter melts.

Transfer the mussels and cooking liquid to a large serving bowl. Serve family style with crusty bread.

Walking along the coast, I often see mussels and seaweed thriving in the same areas. The bivalves clean the ocean and the seaweed feeds and shelters many of its critters. Just as these two belong together in nature, they make well-matched partners in this simple dish. A little sour cream enriches the broth and tempers the spice of the chili flakes.

MUSSELS IN CREAMY, SPICY SEAWEED BROTH

3 lb live mussels
4 Tbsp (½ stick) unsalted butter (divided)
2 shallots, finely chopped
1 tsp sea salt
¼ cup white wine
1 tsp chili flakes
½ cup crumbled dried seaweed such as kelp or nori
½ cup roughly chopped blanched sea asparagus (optional, see Notes)
½ cup sour cream (optional)
Zest and juice of 1 lime
Crusty artisan bread, to serve

Rinse the mussels under cold water, and discard any that are open and won't close when tapped or that have broken shells. Scrub off any debris and pull off the beard.

Melt 3 tablespoons of the butter in a large pot over medium heat. Add the shallots and salt, and sauté for 5 minutes or until tender and translucent. Add the wine and chili flakes and bring to a boil. Add the mussels, cover, and cook for 2 minutes or until the mussels just open. (Do not overcook. Mussels cook very quickly. You know they're ready when the shells are open.) Discard any that don't open.

Stir in the seaweed, and the sea asparagus and sour cream if using. Add the lime zest and juice and the remaining 1 tablespoon of butter, stirring until it melts. Transfer the mussels and cooking liquid to a large serving bowl. Serve family style with crusty bread.

CHEF'S NOTES: Sea asparagus, also known as Salicornia, sea beans, pickleweed, and samphire, is a shoreline plant with a pleasing snappy crunch and lightly salty taste. It looks like a succulent plant crossed with tiny asparagus. Find it at well-stocked fish counters or at farmers' markets. Or forage for it yourself in areas where oysters grow—they like the same conditions. To blanch it, immerse in a pot of boiling salted water for about 30 seconds, then plunge in ice water to stop the cooking.

When creating new dishes, I love taking one ingredi-ent—in this case, fennel—and playing with it in differ-ent ways. Here I cook the fresh bulb slowly to bring out its charred and caramelized anise notes, before mix-ing it with rich cream, chunky potatoes, and steamed mussels. Just before serving I dust each bowl of chow-der with fennel pollen, which you can buy in specialty food stores. It echoes the anise flavor, but adds its own summery hints of citrus and marshmallow.

MUSSELS

3 lb live mussels
3 Tbsp olive oil
1 shallot, thinly sliced
2 cloves garlic, crushed
1 cup white wine or craft beer (not too hoppy)

CHOWDER

¼ cup olive oil
1 large bulb fennel, diced
¼ cup (½ stick) unsalted butter
1 onion, chopped
2 stalks celery, chopped
2 cloves garlic, chopped
1 Tbsp sea salt
1 tsp coarsely ground black pepper
1 cup white wine or craft beer (not too hoppy)
2 cups whipping cream
2 cups whole milk
¾ lb Yukon gold potatoes, peeled and diced
1 cup fresh or frozen corn kernels
1 Tbsp extra-virgin olive oil, to drizzle
2 Tbsp pure maple syrup, to drizzle
½ tsp fennel pollen, for garnish (see Notes on page 51)
3 Tbsp chopped fresh chives, for garnish

SERVES 4

MUSSEL AND MAPLE CHOWDER WITH CARAMELIZED FENNEL AND POLLEN

MUSSELS Rinse the mussels under cold water, and discard any that are open and won't close when tapped or that have broken shells. Scrub off any debris and pull off the beard.

Heat the olive oil in a large pot over medium heat. Add the shallots, and sauté for 3 minutes or until softened. Add the garlic and sauté for another minute. Add the wine (or beer) and bring to a boil. Add the mussels, cover, and cook for about 2 minutes or until the shells just open up. (Do not overcook. Mussels cook very quickly. You know they're ready when the shells are open.) Use a slot-ted spoon to transfer the mussels to a baking sheet to cool. Discard any that are unopened.

Strain the cooking liquid through a fine-mesh sieve and reserve. Remove the mussels from their shells and place in a bowl.

CHOWDER Heat the olive oil in a large sauce-pan over medium heat. Add the fennel and sauté until golden brown, about 10 minutes. Transfer to a plate.

Return the saucepan to medium heat and melt the butter. Add the onions and cel-ery, and sauté for 7 minutes or until onions are tender and translucent. Add the garlic and salt and pepper, and sauté for another minute until fragrant. Pour in the wine (or beer), stirring to scrape up the browned bits. Cook for 2 to 3 minutes or until the liquid is mostly evaporated. Add the cream, milk, and reserved mussel cooking liquid, and simmer for 20 minutes.

Add the potatoes and corn and cook for 10 minutes or until tender. Add the mussels and cook until heated through. Taste and adjust seasoning with more salt and pepper if desired.

Ladle the chowder into 4 serving bowls, drizzle each with olive oil and maple syrup, and garnish with a sprinkle of fennel pollen and chives.

When you take the time to cook garlic and onions low and slow, beautiful things happen. They become sweet, tender, and luscious—and offer incredible depth of flavor to simple dishes like this. If you caramelize the onions and confit the garlic ahead of time—say, on the weekend when you're puttering around the house—this fragrant stew, with its crusty garlic toasts slathered with chopped briny olives, comes together in no time.

SERVES 4

MUSSEL STEW WITH GARLIC CONFIT, CARAMELIZED ONIONS, AND OLIVE TOAST

GARLIC CONFIT Combine the garlic, oil, and rosemary in a small saucepan. Add more oil if necessary to ensure the cloves are covered. Set over low heat and cook for 20 minutes or until cloves are tender and just lightly browned. (Do not boil as this will roast the garlic too quickly.) Remove the pan from the heat and set aside to cool. (The oil will keep refrigerated for up to 4 days. Use the extra for brushing bread before toasting or grilling, in vinaigrettes, and for finishing roasted fish.)

OLIVE TOAST Preheat the broiler and set the oven rack to the topmost position.

Pulse the olives in a blender or food processor into a coarse puree. (Alternatively, use a knife to finely chop.)

Brush one side of each bread slice with garlic oil from the garlic confit. Set on a baking sheet and broil for 1 to 2 minutes or until golden brown. Top each toast with a spoonful of the chopped olives.

MUSSELS Rinse the mussels under cold water, and discard any that are open and won't close when tapped or that have broken shells. Scrub off any debris and pull off the beard.

Heat the oil in a large pot over medium-low heat. Add the onions and sauté for 20 to 30 minutes, stirring frequently, until onions turn a deep golden brown. (As the moisture cooks off, the onions will begin to caramelize.) They should taste sweet and salty, like onion caramel.

Increase the heat to medium. Add half the confit garlic cloves and 2 tablespoons of garlic oil, and sauté for 2 minutes. Add the tomatoes and cook for 5 minutes or until softened.

Add the water, bring to a boil over medium-high heat, then add the mussels. Cover and cook for 2 to 3 minutes or until the mussels have opened. (Do not overcook. Mussels cook very quickly. You know they're ready when the shells are open.) Remove the pot from the heat and discard any that are unopened.

Stir in the parsley and lemon zest and juice. Transfer to a large serving bowl. Serve family style or in individual bowls with the grilled olive toasts. Pass the remaining confit garlic cloves at the table, for adding to the stew or smashing on the toasts.

GARLIC CONFIT
20 peeled cloves garlic
1 cup olive oil, plus extra if needed
1 sprig rosemary

OLIVE TOAST
2 cups Niçoise or kalamata olives, pitted
4 thick slices crusty artisan bread

MUSSELS
2 lb live mussels
3 Tbsp olive oil
2 red onions, thinly sliced
2 Tbsp garlic oil from garlic confit (see above)
1 cup whole cherry tomatoes
½ cup cold water
3 Tbsp chopped flat-leaf parsley
Zest and juice of 1 lemon

NED'S SEAFOOD AND SHELLFISH TACKLE BOX

Traditionally, a tackle box is a container for all your fishing gear: hooks, lines, sinkers, floats, baits, and reels, but I like to use it as a vessel for playful and visually stunning seafood displays for dinner parties. I simply fill it with crushed ice and my favorite fish and shellfish dishes and sauces. The preparation requires some time and patience, but you'll have tons of fun working on the presentation.

CLAMS WITH CHEF'S JUICE
(34)

PACIFIC OYSTERS
(142)

KELP AND SMOKED SEA SALT SCONES
(172)

MUSSEL SALAD WITH ORANGES, OLIVES, AND SMOKED PAPRIKA
(129)

SCALLOP CRUDO
(148)

CHILLED
SHRIMP

CHILI LIME
MAYO
(60)

BAKED
WONTON CHIPS
(126)

LEMON
VINAIGRETTE
(77)

TUNA
TATAKI
(103)

DUNGENESS
CRABMEAT
(116 for steam-
ing instructions)

137

Rich and robust, octopus demands other powerful ingredients as complements. Romesco—a Catalan dipping sauce made with roasted bell peppers and crunchy Marcona almonds—fits the bill. Once the octopus is prepped, just a quick char on the grill crisps up the exterior and brings out its bold flavor.

ROMESCO SAUCE
8 red bell peppers
5 Tbsp olive oil
½ cup Marcona almonds
Sea salt and coarsely
    ground black pepper

VEGETABLE STOCK
4 quarts water
1 bulb fennel, diced
1 onion, diced
3 stalks celery, chopped
2 lemons, halved
5 cloves garlic, crushed
2 bay leaves
2 sprigs thyme

OCTOPUS
3 lb octopus (a whole
    octopus, cleaned, or just
    the tentacles; see Notes)
1 lb pickling or other coarse
    salt, for scrubbing
½ cup coarse kosher salt
¼ cup granulated sugar
2 cups water
¼ cup extra-virgin olive oil,
    plus extra to drizzle
Sea salt and coarsely
    ground black pepper
Romaine hearts, roughly
    chopped, to serve
Marcona almonds, for
    garnish
Zest and juice of 1 lemon,
    to serve

GRILLED OCTOPUS WITH ROMESCO, MARCONA ALMONDS, AND ROMAINE HEARTS

ROMESCO SAUCE Preheat the oven to 400°F. Line a baking sheet with aluminum foil, put the peppers on the sheet, and roast for 10 to 12 minutes. Turn them over and roast for another 10 to 12 minutes, or until the skin is charred and soft. Set aside until cool enough to handle. Peel off the skins, slice peppers open to remove the seeds, and slice.

Transfer three-quarters of the peppers to a blender or food processor (the remaining peppers will be used in the salad), and add the olive oil and almonds. Puree until smooth. Season with salt and pepper to taste. (Romesco sauce can be made several days ahead and refrigerated.)

VEGETABLE STOCK Combine all the ingredients in a large pot. Bring to a boil, reduce the heat, and simmer for 25 minutes. Strain the stock, discarding the solids, and return it to the pot.

OCTOPUS Scrub the octopus with a third of the pickling salt to remove the slime. Rinse thoroughly. Repeat this procedure twice. Place the octopus in a nonreactive container, and add the salt, sugar, and 2 cups water. Cover and refrigerate for 12 hours. Rinse.

Bring the pot of vegetable stock (or water) to a boil. Add the brined octopus, reduce the heat to medium-low, and simmer for 1 to 1½ hours or until a knife slides in and out of the flesh easily. Drain and allow to cool. Using a paper towel, wipe off the purple skin but leave the suckers. (Octopus can be prepared a day ahead and refrigerated.)

Preheat the grill to high heat. Clean and oil the cooking grate. In a large bowl, toss the octopus with the olive oil and season with salt and pepper. Grill the octopus, turning, for about 4 minutes or until crispy and charred all over but still moist.

Slice the octopus into ¼-inch disks. Arrange the romaine and peppers on a plate and scatter the octopus over it. Dollop Romesco sauce around the plate. Garnish with the almonds. Squeeze the lemon juice over all, drizzle with olive oil, and sprinkle with sea salt and lemon zest.

CHEF'S NOTES: A whole fresh octopus might seem intimidating to cook at home, but I assure you it's simple. The trick is getting the muscles and tough connective tissues to tenderize. Freezing and then defrosting helps move things along by breaking down the creature's cellular structure, so don't shy away from frozen octopus. But soaking the legs in brine will relax the protein fibers, too. Then give them a long, slow simmer to soften the connective tissue into a silky gelatin.

My good friend and sustainable-seafood mentor Chef Rob Clark was famous for his octopus bacon at C restaurant in Vancouver. He understood that people will try unusual seafood species if they're prepared in familiar ways or served with more familiar ingredients. That's the rationale behind this dish, which pairs Chef Clark's unusual bacon with seared scallops drizzled in an almost toffee-flavored vinaigrette.

OCTOPUS BACON

12 lb octopus, thoroughly washed (see Notes)
2 lb pickling or other coarse salt, for scrubbing
1 cup coarse kosher salt
½ cup granulated sugar
4 cups water
2 cups maple chips soaked in water
About 4 cups canola oil

BROWN BUTTER AND SHERRY VINAIGRETTE

¼ cup (½ stick) unsalted butter
2 Tbsp aged sherry vinegar
1 Tbsp Dijon mustard
1 tsp honey
¼ tsp sea salt
¼ tsp coarsely ground black pepper
¼ cup canola oil

SERVES 4

OCTOPUS BACON WITH PAN-SEARED SCALLOPS, BROWN BUTTER, AND SHERRY VINEGAR

OCTOPUS BACON Scrub the octopus with a third of the pickling salt to remove the slime. Rinse thoroughly. Repeat this procedure twice. Place the octopus in a nonreactive container, and add the 1 cup kosher salt, sugar, and water. Cover and refrigerate for 12 hours. Rinse.

Heat the soaked maple chips in a smoker set at low heat, add the octopus, and cold-smoke for 2 hours.

Place the smoked octopus in a large but tight-fitting pot, add enough oil to cover, and cook over medium heat for 1½ to 2 hours or until tender. Set aside to cool.

When cool enough to handle, drain and reserve the oil. Wearing rubber gloves, remove the suction cups from the tentacles by running your closed hand down the arm from the head to the tips. Cut the arms into 6- to 8-inch lengths. If not using right away, pack into an airtight container, add enough of its cooking oil to cover it, and refrigerate. (Stored this way it will keep for several weeks).

VINAIGRETTE Melt the butter in a small saucepan over low heat. Allow the butter to gently simmer for about 5 minutes or until the milk solids turn golden brown and fall to the bottom of the pan. Transfer to a bowl to stop the cooking.

Combine the vinegar, mustard, honey, and salt and pepper in a small bowl. While whisking, slowly drizzle the oil and brown butter in a thin steady stream until incorporated and the mixture is emulsified. Adjust seasoning to taste. (Alternatively, you can do this with an immersion blender or in a blender or small food processor. Can be made ahead of time; will keep refrigerated for up to 2 weeks.)

PAN-SEARED SCALLOPS
12 scallops
2 Tbsp canola oil
Sea salt
1 Tbsp unsalted butter
1 lemon, halved
Octopus Bacon
  (see page 140)
Arugula or watercress, for
  garnish

PAN-SEARED SCALLOPS If the abductor muscle (a little flap) is still on the side of the scallops, remove it (it gets tough when cooked). Use a paper towel to pat the scallops dry. Heat the oil in a heavy-bottomed skillet over medium-high heat until almost smoking. Season the scallops with salt and add to the skillet, making sure not to crowd them (cook them in batches if necessary). Allow to sear undisturbed for about 2 minutes or until browned. Flip them over, add the butter to the pan, and squeeze the lemon over the scallops. Continue cooking, basting with the buttery juices for 2 minutes or until browned.

Preheat the grill to high. Grill the octopus for about 3 minutes per side or until crisp, then thinly slice. Or slice the octopus into ¼-inch-thick "rashers" and fry in a skillet over medium-high heat for a couple minutes or until crispy. Alternatively, fry the rashers ahead of time and simply rewarm the slices in the cooking oil.

To serve, set 3 scallops on each plate, add a few slices of octopus bacon, add the arugula or watercress, and drizzle over a tablespoon of the brown butter and sherry vinaigrette.

CHEF'S NOTES: The recipe makes more bacon than you need for 4 people, but if you're going to the trouble of making it, you might as well have extra. Store it in an airtight container in the refrigerator, or freeze it. If you're not ready to venture into the realm of cured and smoked octopus, you can serve up a smaller grilled octopus instead (page 138), or just stick to the scallops and vinaigrette, add a fresh salad, and call it a day.

Stuart Brioza, chef-owner of State Bird Provisions and the Progress in San Francisco, created the original dish that inspired this recipe, and it made a huge impression on me. It was for a Northern Chefs Alliance dinner that brought together chefs from the northern half of North America. Initially the U.S. chefs were huddled on one side of the room and the Canadians on the other. But as the hors d'oeuvres were laid out in the middle of the room, we all quickly dropped our guard and bonded over these Hog Island oysters with their sweet-and-sour pickled nori topping. After trying them, I hunted down Stuart so we could geek out over our love of seaweed.

SERVES 4

PICKLED SEAWEED
1 cup water
1 cup white wine vinegar
½ cup sake
¼ cup granulated sugar
2 Tbsp sea salt
2 cups hydrated dried seaweed such as dulse, sea lettuce, and ogo, cut into strips (see Notes)
1 shallot, very thinly sliced

OYSTERS
Crushed ice or rock salt
16 to 24 Pacific oysters

RAW OYSTERS WITH PICKLED SEAWEED

PICKLED SEAWEED In a large saucepan, combine the water, vinegar, sake, sugar, and salt, and bring to a boil over medium-high heat. Transfer to a bowl and set aside to cool. Stir in the seaweed and the shallots, and refrigerate overnight.

OYSTERS Pour a ½-inch deep layer of crushed ice or rock salt on a serving platter. Shuck the oysters, reserving them on their half shell. Nestle the shells into the ice or salt. Top each oyster with the pickled seaweed and shallots and serve.

CHEF'S NOTES: Soak dried seaweed in cold water for about 10 minutes. Fresh seaweed is a superfood that's worth seeking out. Ask your fishmonger to stock it.

A play on oysters Rockefeller, this dish is all about luxury. It's also great for showcasing meatier Pacific oysters, which lend themselves well to grilling or baking because they're large and dense. The silky, buttery béarnaise ramps up their creaminess and bakes up beautifully golden. Don't be surprised by the maple syrup in this dish: I started out as a pastry chef and often introduce a touch of sweetness to heighten the flavors of savory ingredients.

SERVES 4

½ cup (1 stick) unsalted butter
½ small shallot, finely chopped
¼ cup white wine
2 Tbsp white wine vinegar
Sea salt and coarsely ground black pepper
2 egg yolks
1½ tsp maple syrup
1 Tbsp chopped fresh chives, plus extra for garnish
12 Pacific oysters, freshly shucked and reserved on their half shell
Rock salt, for positioning the oysters

BAKED OYSTERS WITH MAPLE BÉARNAISE

Melt the butter in a small saucepan over medium heat. Allow to simmer, spooning off the white froth as it rises to the surface, until there's no more froth and the milk solids accumulate on the bottom and sides of the pan. Remove the pan from the heat and let the solids settle for a few minutes. Pour off the clear, golden butter into a measuring cup, leaving the solids behind (you can also use a fine-mesh sieve or cheesecloth-lined strainer).

Wipe out the saucepan and add the shallots, wine, vinegar, and salt and pepper. Bring to a boil over high heat, reduce to medium heat, and simmer until the liquid is reduced to 2 tablespoons. Remove the pan from the heat and allow to cool.

Fill a saucepan with a couple inches of water. Bring to a simmer over medium-high heat, then reduce to low. Set a stainless-steel bowl over the simmering water and add the egg yolks. Whisk the egg yolks until doubled in volume, about 3 minutes. While whisking, slowly add the clarified butter, a little at a time, until fully incorporated and emulsified. Remove the bowl from the heat and whisk in the reserved shallot reduction. Adjust the seasoning with salt and pepper to taste, and stir in the maple syrup and chives.

Preheat the oven to 375°F. Pour a ½-inch deep layer of rock salt onto a rimmed baking sheet. Nestle the oysters in their half shell onto the salt. Cover each oyster with a spoonful of sauce. Bake for 10 minutes or until the oysters are cooked and the béarnaise sauce is golden brown. Sprinkle over some chives and serve immediately.

½ cup (1 stick) unsalted butter, softened
½ Tbsp chopped flat-leaf parsley
½ Tbsp smoked sea salt (see Notes)
½ Tbsp honey
1 Tbsp craft beer (not too hoppy)
2 dozen Pacific oysters

SERVES 4 TO 6

GRILLED OYSTERS WITH BEER, SMOKED SALT, AND HONEY BUTTER

In the bowl of a stand mixer or using a hand-held mixer, beat the butter, parsley, salt, and honey on medium-high speed. Scrape down the sides of the bowl. On medium speed, beat in the beer, a little at a time, until fully incorporated.

Scrape the mixture onto a sheet of plastic wrap. Fold the plastic over the butter and shape and roll it into a 2-inch-diameter log. Chill in the refrigerator for at least 2 hours or until firm.

Preheat the grill to medium-high heat. Shuck the oysters, reserving them on their half shell. Slice the butter into ¼-inch-thick disks. Set a disk of butter on top of each oyster, and grill for about 5 minutes or until the oysters are just cooked and firm and butter is melted and bubbly.

CHEF'S NOTES: Smoked sea salt is sea salt that has been cold-smoked over fragrant wood. It's great for adding a smoky note to dishes. You can find smoked sea salt from gourmet markets and online retailers.

This salad is inspired by the sublime lime pickles that my friend Stuart Brioza has on the menu at his restaurant State Bird Provisions in San Francisco. His need nine months to ferment, but I've taken a few shortcuts so mine are ready within a couple of days. They're incredible for livening up sweet seared scallops, and they're similarly delicious chopped up and added to salad dressings, vegetable sautés, or even cooked lentils.

SERVES 4

SCALLOP SALAD WITH LIME PICKLE AND CASHEWS

LIME PICKLE Rub the salt into the limes. Transfer to an airtight container and let sit for 2 days in a cool dry place.

Heat the oil in a small saucepan over medium heat, add the mustard seeds, peppercorns, coriander, and cumin. Cook for about 30 seconds or until fragrant and mustard seeds begin to pop. Add the salted limes and lime juice, vinegar, brown sugar, garlic, and chili powder. Cover and cook for 1 hour or until the limes are tender. Set aside to cool, then transfer to a sterilized jar. Be sure all the solids are submerged in the liquid (add more lime juice if necessary). Refrigerate for at least 3 days before using. (Will keep for several months refrigerated.)

LIME VINAIGRETTE Combine the lime zest and juice, mustard, and salt in a small bowl. While whisking, slowly drizzle the canola oil in a thin steady stream until incorporated and the mixture is emulsified. Adjust seasoning to taste. (Alternatively, you can do this with an immersion blender or in a blender or small food processor.) Can be made ahead of time; will keep refrigerated for up to 2 weeks (although the lime flavor will start to weaken after a few days).

SCALLOPS If the abductor muscle (a little flap) is still on the side of the scallops, remove it (it gets tough when cooked).

Heat the oil in a heavy-bottomed skillet over medium-high heat until almost smoking. Use a paper towel to pat the scallops dry. Season with salt. Add the scallops to the skillet, making sure not to crowd them (cook them in batches if necessary). Allow to sear undisturbed for about 2 minutes or until browned. Flip them over, add the butter to the pan, and squeeze the lime over. Continue cooking, basting with the buttery juices, for 2 minutes or until browned.

In a bowl, toss the lettuce with just enough vinaigrette to coat. Divide salad among each plate. Sprinkle each with 1 tablespoon diced lime pickle and 2 tablespoons cashews. Add 3 seared scallops and a tablespoon of raisins.

LIME PICKLE
12 limes, cut into wedges
1 cup kosher salt
2 Tbsp canola oil
3 Tbsp yellow mustard seeds
1 Tbsp black peppercorns
2 tsp coriander seeds
1 tsp cumin seeds
Juice of 6 limes, plus extra if needed
3 Tbsp white wine vinegar
1 cup packed brown sugar
3 cloves garlic, finely chopped
1 tsp chili powder

LIME VINAIGRETTE
Zest and juice of 1½ limes
1 Tbsp Dijon mustard
¼ tsp sea salt
½ cup canola oil

SCALLOPS
12 scallops
2 Tbsp canola oil
Sea salt
1 Tbsp unsalted butter
1 lime, halved
8 cups little gem lettuce, torn
¼ cup diced lime pickle rind (flesh discarded)
½ cup toasted cashews, chopped, for garnish
¼ cup golden raisins, for garnish

ORANGE VINAIGRETTE
Zest and juice of ½ orange
1½ tsp orange juice
    concentrate
2 tsp Dijon mustard
¼ tsp sea salt
¼ tsp coarsely ground black
    pepper
½ cup canola oil

SCALLOP CRUDO
½ cup pine nuts
½ lb scallops
1 avocado, pitted and diced
2 oranges, segmented
1 small red chile, seeded
    and thinly sliced
Zest and juice of 1 lime
Sea salt and coarsely
    ground black pepper
Extra-virgin olive oil, for
    drizzling

SERVES 4

SCALLOP CRUDO WITH CHILES, ORANGES, AVOCADO, AND PINE NUTS

ORANGE VINAIGRETTE Combine the orange zest and juice, concentrate, mustard, salt, and pepper in a small bowl. While whisking, slowly drizzle the oil in a thin steady stream until incorporated and the mixture is emulsified. Adjust seasoning to taste. (Alternatively, you can do this with an immersion blender or in a blender or small food processor.) Can be made ahead of time; will keep refrigerated for up to 2 weeks (although the orange flavor will start to weaken after a few days).

SCALLOP CRUDO Heat a small skillet over medium-low heat. Add the pine nuts and toast, stirring frequently, for 3 to 5 minutes or until golden brown. Transfer to a plate to cool, then coarsely crush.

If the abductor muscle (a little flap) is still on the side of the scallops, remove it (it gets tough when cooked). Slice each scallop in half crosswise into 2 disks. Spoon about ½ cup of the orange vinaigrette onto a serving platter. Arrange the scallops, avocado, and orange segments on top. Sprinkle with the sliced chiles, lime zest, and salt and pepper to taste. Drizzle everything with lime juice, a little olive oil, and a few more tablespoons of orange vinaigrette. Garnish with the pine nuts.

Weathervane scallops are large wild scallops harvested in Alaska. These scallops have a sweet flavor and steaklike texture that's firmer than the smaller bay scallops. While this recipe calls for grapefruit, you can experiment with other types of citrus, such as tangerines or lime. If you're looking for an even bolder hit of herbs, the fresh thyme in the brown butter could be switched out for rosemary—these meaty scallops can take it.

SERVES 4

6 Tbsp (¾ stick) unsalted butter
1 tsp chopped fresh thyme or rosemary
1 grapefruit or pomelo
12 Weathervane scallops
Sea salt and coarsely ground black pepper
1 bunch watercress, stems removed
Flaked sea salt, to sprinkle

ROASTED SCALLOPS WITH GRAPEFRUIT, BROWN BUTTER, AND THYME

Melt the butter in a small saucepan over low heat. Add the thyme (or rosemary). Allow the butter to gently simmer for about 5 minutes or until the milk solids turn golden brown and fall to the bottom of the pan.

Meanwhile, use a sharp knife to cut the peel and white pith off the grapefruit (or pomelo). Working over a bowl, cut between the membranes to remove the segments and let them fall into the bowl. Squeeze the membranes over the bowl to extract all the juice before discarding.

If the abductor muscle (a little flap) is still on the side of the scallops, remove it. (It toughens when cooked.)

Heat a heavy-bottomed skillet over medium-high heat for 1 to 2 minutes. Add 2 tablespoons of the brown butter (aim to use the clarified liquid, not the brown bits). Pat the scallops dry and add to the pan, making sure not to crowd them (cook them in batches if necessary). Allow to sear undisturbed for about 2 minutes or until browned. Season with salt and pepper, flip the scallops over, and add the remaining brown butter, this time making sure to add all the brown bits. Add 2 tablespoons of the grapefruit (or pomelo) juice. Allow the scallops to sear for another 2 minutes on the other side or until browned, basting them with the liquid in the pan.

Divide the watercress among 4 plates. Set the scallops on top and garnish with grapefruit segments. Drizzle with the pan sauce and sprinkle with flaked sea salt.

Sea urchin isn't something that most people think to cook on a Tuesday evening, but I urge the adventurous home cook to try it. Imagine crème brûlée infused with the flavors of the ocean. The silkiness of this sea urchin custard and its distinctive umami notes make it an unforgettable seafood experience. And on the side, shamrock-green and crunchy sea asparagus, in a salsa verde, creates colorful contrast. This would make a wonderful first course or a simple brunch dish, served with a butter lettuce salad.

SERVES 6

SEA URCHIN CUSTARD
6 eggs
3 egg yolks
1 cup uni (about 15 to 18)
4 cups whole milk
1 tsp sea salt
½ cup chilled pink shrimp (cooked and peeled), for garnish

DULSE AND SEA ASPARAGUS SALSA VERDE
½ cup finely chopped dried dulse, soaked (see Notes)
¼ cup finely chopped fresh chives
¼ cup chopped flat-leaf parsley
¼ cup chopped blanched sea asparagus (see Notes on page 131)
1 tsp coarsely ground black pepper
¼ tsp chili flakes
Zest and juice of ½ lime
¼ cup extra-virgin olive oil

SEA URCHIN CUSTARD WITH DULSE AND SEA ASPARAGUS SALSA VERDE

SEA URCHIN CUSTARD Preheat the oven to 300°F. Bring a kettle of water to a boil. Whisk the eggs and egg yolks in a medium bowl. Finely chop the uni and whisk into the eggs until combined. Whisk in the milk and salt.

Place 6 ramekins or custard cups in a small roasting pan. Divide the uni mixture among each cup. Create a water bath by adding enough hot water to fill the pan halfway up the sides of the ramekins. Bake for 30 minutes or until the custard is set. Remove from the oven, allow to cool, and chill in the refrigerator.

SALSA VERDE Drain the seaweed, then combine all the ingredients together.

Top the sea urchin custards with shrimp and serve with the seaweed salsa verde.

CHEF'S NOTES: Dried dulse is quickly gaining popularity as a salty, umami-rich ingredient that's delicious in everything from salads to stir-fries. It's often even fried up as a bacon substitute. Before using, inspect the dulse for tiny shells and give it a quick rinse under cold water.

Delicate, creamy, and exceptionally rich, sea urchin stands up well to bold flavors. I serve Japanese rice on the side: as any sushi chef will tell you, this warm and sticky, subtly sweet short-grained variety is the best rice to serve with seafood, and properly cooked Japanese rice is definitely worth mastering.

BLACK GARLIC, MISO, AND TANGERINE VINAIGRETTE

¼ head black garlic or roasted garlic cloves (see Notes)

2 tsp red miso

2 tsp honey or maple syrup

1 Tbsp Dijon mustard

Juice of ½ tangerine or blood orange

½ tsp sea salt, plus extra to taste

¾ cup canola oil

SUSHI RICE AND SEA URCHIN

2 cups Japanese sushi rice

2 cups cold water, for cooking the rice

2 Tbsp sweetened rice wine vinegar

12 sea urchins

½ cup finely chopped cucumber, for garnish

Sliced scallions, for garnish

Toasted sesame seeds, for garnish

SERVES 4

SEA URCHIN WITH SUSHI RICE AND BLACK GARLIC, MISO, AND TANGERINE VINAIGRETTE

VINAIGRETTE Combine the garlic, miso, honey (or maple syrup), mustard, citrus juice, and salt in a medium bowl. While whisking, slowly drizzle the oil in a thin steady stream until incorporated and the mixture is emulsified. Adjust seasoning to taste. (Alternatively, you can do this with an immersion blender or in a blender or small food processor.) Can be made ahead of time; will keep refrigerated for up to 2 weeks.

SUSHI RICE AND SEA URCHIN Rinse the rice in several changes of water until the water is clear. In a saucepan, combine the rice with the water, and bring to a boil over high heat. Reduce to low, cover, and cook for 15 minutes or until the liquid is absorbed. Remove the pan from the heat and let stand for 15 minutes.

Transfer the rice to a large mixing bowl, and sprinkle over some of the vinegar. Stir the rice and sprinkle more of the vinegar, a little at a time while turning the rice over to ensure all the rice gets coated. Keep warm.

Scoop the rice into 4 small bowls, top with 3 pieces of sea urchin and the vinaigrette, and garnish with the cucumber, scallions, and sesame seeds.

CHEF'S NOTES: Black garlic is a caramelized garlic that's slightly matte black and gooey in texture. With the sweetness of molasses and dark caramel combined with umami notes, it has a rich, layered, and intense flavor. It can be found at specialty Asian food stores. If you're substituting regular roasted garlic, see the Notes on page 125 for instructions.

Warm and freshly toasted slices of fluffy brioche or challah are the perfect vehicles for delicate spot prawns doused in vanilla-and-lime-infused butter. This dish makes an excellent first course or brunch starter and only takes minutes to prepare. If you peel the shrimp yourself, save the heads and shells to make a quick batch of shrimp stock to use in things like seafood-based soups, chowders, and risottos.

SERVES 4

2 Tbsp canola oil
1½ lb fresh or thawed spot prawns, heads and tails removed, peeled and deveined
2 Tbsp unsalted butter
1 lime, halved
¼ tsp lime zest
1 vanilla bean, split lengthwise and seeds scraped
Sea salt
8 slices brioche or challah bread
2 Tbsp chopped fresh chives, for garnish

SPOT PRAWN TOAST WITH VANILLA LIME BUTTER

Heat the oil in a medium skillet over medium heat, add the spot prawns, and cook, tossing, for 10 seconds. (Work in batches if necessary to ensure all the prawns come in direct contact with the pan.)

Add the butter to the pan and squeeze the lime over all. Add the vanilla seeds to the pan. Toss the prawns with the buttery juices for another 20 seconds or until just cooked through. Transfer prawns and pan juices to a serving bowl and season with salt.

Lightly toast the bread in a toaster or under a broiler, and divide among plates. Top each with the prawns and spoon the pan juices on top. Garnish with a sprinkle of chives.

The first recipe I ever made as a 19-year-old culinary student was a Caesar salad dressing of roasted garlic and rosemary. My mother, brother, and sister loved it so much that I must have made it every week for a year after that. And now each time I smell the aroma of roasting garlic, it takes me right back. This shrimp Caesar salad pays homage to that exciting time in my life, when I was just starting to develop a reverence for great ingredients. It brings together the sweet tenderness of shrimp, the crunch of romaine hearts, and the zing and subtle caramelized notes of grilled lemons.

SERVES 4

SHRIMP CAESAR WITH GRILLED LEMON

CAESAR VINAIGRETTE Preheat the oven to 400°F. Slice the top third off of the garlic head to expose the cloves. Set on a sheet of aluminum foil and drizzle with a little of the olive oil. Wrap in the foil and roast for 30 to 40 minutes or until cloves are soft.

Meanwhile, heat the ¾ cup olive oil and the rosemary in a small saucepan set over medium heat. Bring to a simmer, then remove the pan from the heat and set aside for 20 minutes or until the rosemary is infused into the oil. Remove rosemary and discard.

Squeeze half the roasted garlic out of the papery skins into a blender or food processor. Add the vinegar, both mustards, anchovy, lemon zest and juice, and ½ cup of the rosemary oil (set aside the remaining ¼ cup for the croutons). Stir in the olive oil mayo and season with the salt and pepper, adjusting to taste. Blend for about 1 minute until emulsified. (Dressing can be made ahead and refrigerated for up to 3 days. Leftover roasted garlic can be added to any tasty mash.)

CROUTONS Preheat the oven to 375°F. In a bowl, brush the bread slices with rosemary oil until evenly coated. Season lightly with salt and pepper. Spread on a rimmed baking sheet and toast in the oven, stirring occasionally to promote even browning, for 15 minutes or until golden. Tear into pieces.

SALAD Heat a skillet over medium-high heat (or preheat the grill). Brush the cut sides of the lemons with olive oil. Place cut side down onto the pan (or grill), and sear for 2 to 4 minutes or until caramelized and golden.

In a large bowl, toss the romaine and half the croutons with enough dressing to coat. Squeeze the caramelized lemons over the bowl. Season with salt and pepper to taste and toss again.

Transfer the salad to a serving bowl or platter. Arrange the shrimp on top. Sprinkle the Parmesan over the salad. Garnish with the remaining croutons and anchovies.

CAESAR VINAIGRETTE
1 head garlic
¾ cup olive oil (divided), plus extra for drizzling the garlic
1 sprig rosemary
2½ Tbsp red wine vinegar
1½ Tbsp Dijon mustard
1½ tsp whole grain mustard
1 oil-packed anchovy
Zest and juice of 1 lemon
½ cup Olive Oil Mayonnaise (page 35)
1 tsp sea salt
½ tsp coarsely ground black pepper

CROUTONS
½ sourdough baguette or other artisan bread, cut into ½-inch-thick slices
¼ cup rosemary oil (see above)
Sea salt and coarsely ground black pepper

SALAD
½ cup finely grated Parmesan
1 lemon, halved
Olive oil, for brushing
2 romaine hearts, leaves separated
Sea salt and coarsely ground black pepper
½ lb chilled pink shrimp (cooked and peeled)
8 white marinated anchovies, for garnish

1 lb fresh or thawed spot prawns, heads and tails removed, peeled and deveined
3 Tbsp extra-virgin olive oil
Juice of 3 limes
Juice of 1 pomelo
1 pomelo, segmented
½ Thai bird chile, seeded and thinly sliced
Sea salt and coarsely ground black pepper
2 avocadoes
¼ cup fresh cilantro leaves
Corn chips or Wonton Chips (page 126)

SERVES 4 TO 6

SPOT PRAWN CEVICHE WITH POMELO, LIME, AND CHILE

Cut the prawns into bite-size pieces. In a medium bowl, combine the prawns, olive oil, lime juice (reserve ½ tablespoon), pomelo juice, and pomelo segments. Add the chile and salt and pepper to taste. (Use the chiles sparingly—you only want a subtle amount of heat.) Set aside for 10 minutes to marinate.

Cut the avocadoes in half lengthwise and remove the pit. Scoop the flesh into a medium bowl. Using a fork, coarsely mash the avocado, add the reserved lime juice, and season with salt and pepper to taste. Spread the avocado in the bottom of a wide shallow serving bowl.

Spoon the spot prawns and their liquid on top of the crushed avocado. Garnish with the cilantro and serve with corn chips or crispy wontons.

Pink shrimp (sometimes called bay shrimp or Oregon shrimp) are tiny, delicate, and sweet, and they're always sold precooked, which makes it easy to put these messy yet spectacularly delicious sandwiches together. Hot dog buns are quite traditional on the East Coast, but I think these deserve a step up into the buttery brioche-bread category. Cut pockets into thick slices and toast them, buttered, in a skillet until golden. Stuff them with the shrimp and dig in while they're still warm.

SERVES 4

4 (1½-inch-thick) slices brioche, or 4 brioche buns
2 Tbsp unsalted butter, softened
1 lb pink shrimp (cooked and peeled)
½ cup Chili Lime Mayo (page 60)
1 lime or lemon
Sea salt and coarsely ground black pepper
Flaked sea salt, to sprinkle
2 Tbsp chopped fresh chives, to sprinkle

SHRIMP ROLL WITH CHILI LIME MAYO

Cut the bread slices in half crosswise, then partially slice each half open so it opens up like a hot dog bun. If using buns, slice horizontally but not all the way through.

Heat a large skillet over medium-high heat. Spread the soft butter on the outside of the bread, and toast in the pan until golden brown and lightly crispy on both sides.

In a medium bowl, mix the shrimp with the Chili Lime Mayo (just enough so the shrimp is lightly coated). Squeeze in the lime (or lemon) juice and salt and pepper to taste.

Spoon the shrimp mixture into the brioche pockets, filling them as much as you can (there is never too much!). Sprinkle with flaked sea salt and chives.

I often make this simple, warming pasta dish for my own family. Garganelli is my preferred pasta for the sauce because the shapes are like little handkerchiefs that have been rolled over and pinched together, with a hole through the middle to trap the sauce's rich garlic flavor. For the shrimp, I reach for the sidestripe variety harvested from Alaska, where the cold waters contribute to its sweet flavor.

SERVES 4

GARGANELLI WITH SHRIMP, GARLIC CONFIT, PEAS, AND CHILI

GARLIC CONFIT Combine the garlic and olive oil in a small saucepan. Add more oil if necessary to ensure the cloves are covered. Set over low heat and cook 20 minutes or until cloves are tender and just lightly browned. (Do not boil as this will roast the garlic too quickly.) Remove the pan from the heat and set aside to cool. (The oil will keep refrigerated for up to 4 days. Use the extra for brushing bread before toasting or grilling, in vinaigrettes, and for finishing roasted fish.)

GARGANELLI Bring a large pot of water to a boil over high heat and salt generously. Add the pasta and cook until al dente, according to manufacturer's instructions. Drain the pasta.

Heat the 2 tablespoons garlic oil in a large skillet over medium heat. Add the shallots and 1 teaspoon salt, and sauté for 30 seconds or until fragrant. Add the shrimp and cook for another 10 seconds or until it starts to turn pink. Add the wine, tomato puree, tomatoes, and confit garlic cloves. Cook for 30 seconds or until warmed through. Add the chili flakes, peas, and the lemon zest and juice. Add the pasta and fold everything together. (You don't want this pasta very saucy, just lightly coated in the tomato puree. The flavor of the shrimp and confit garlic should be the stars.)

Transfer to a large serving platter, and sprinkle over the basil (or chives) and Parmesan. Drizzle over more garlic oil.

GARLIC CONFIT
10 peeled cloves garlic
1 cup olive oil

GARGANELLI
1 lb dried garganelli, orecchiette, linguine, or spaghetti
2 Tbsp garlic oil from garlic confit, plus extra for drizzling (see above)
1 small shallot, finely chopped
1 tsp sea salt
1 lb fresh or thawed sidestripe shrimp, or any medium-size sustainably harvested variety, peeled and deveined
2 Tbsp dry white wine
½ cup tomato puree
2 heirloom tomatoes, chopped (optional)
1 tsp chili flakes
½ cup fresh or frozen peas
Zest and juice of ½ lemon
Fresh basil or chives, chopped, for garnish
Grated Parmesan, to sprinkle

As summer makes way for fall, ease into the chillier evenings with this soothing risotto. It's loaded with sidestripe shrimp, corn, and cheddar—and there's a splash of chili oil for kick. Perfect risotto requires patience. The broth is added little by little as you stir continuously. This coaxes out the natural starches from the rice and creates a creamy "sauce." Just pour yourself a glass of wine and settle in at the warm stove. Your patience will be rewarded with carb-induced bliss.

CHILI OIL

1 cup olive oil
1 Tbsp chili flakes
1 red jalapeño or other red
    chile pepper, seeded and
    diced

SHRIMP RISOTTO

1 lb fresh or thawed
    sidestripe shrimp,
    unpeeled
6 cups Vegetable Stock
    (page 138)
Sea salt and coarsely
    ground black pepper
1 Tbsp canola oil
3 Tbsp Chili Oil (see above)
1 shallot, chopped
2 cups arborio rice
½ cup white wine
½ cup drained and rinsed
    canned white hominy
½ cup fresh or frozen corn
    kernels
½ cup grated white cheddar
2 Tbsp unsalted butter
3 Tbsp finely chopped flat-
    leaf parsley
Flavorful extra-virgin olive
    oil, for drizzling
Zest of 1 lemon, for garnish

SERVES 6

SHRIMP RISOTTO WITH GOLDEN CORN, WHITE CHEDDAR, AND CHILI OIL

CHILI OIL Combine all the ingredients in a small saucepan, and simmer over medium heat for 5 minutes or until the oil looks a bit red and chili is tender. Set aside to cool, then refrigerate. (You can strain the oil if you like. The oil will keep refrigerated for 1 month. Use the extra as a dip for bread or a spicy drizzle over pastas.)

SHRIMP RISOTTO Bring a pot of water to a simmer over medium heat. Add the shrimp, remove the pot from the heat, and allow the shrimp to poach in the water while it cools. (You don't want to cook them: just gently poach them.) Once cool enough to handle, peel and devein the shrimp.

Meanwhile, heat the vegetable stock in a saucepan set over medium-low heat. Season with salt and pepper to taste. Cover and keep warm.

Heat the chili oil in a large skillet over medium heat, add the shallots, season with salt, and cook for 5 minutes or until softened and translucent. Stir in the rice and cook for 2 to 3 minutes or until the rice is coated in the oil and lightly toasted. Pour in the wine and cook for 30 seconds or until almost completely absorbed.

Add just enough warm broth to cover the rice. Stirring continuously, allow to gently simmer until broth is almost completely absorbed (reduce the heat to medium-low if the broth is simmering too quickly). Repeat with the remaining broth, adding it a ladleful at a time, stirring continuously, and letting the rice absorb the broth before adding more. Continue until all the broth is used and the rice is tender, about 20 to 30 minutes.

Stir in the hominy, corn kernels, and cooked shrimp. Cook for 1 minute, then add the cheddar, butter, and parsley. (The risotto should be creamy and a bit loose.) Season with more salt and pepper to taste. Divide among shallow bowls, drizzle with olive oil, and sprinkle with lemon zest.

Most of the squid we eat in North America is imported from Asian fisheries with sustainability issues. Make sure you choose squid that's wild-caught off the coast of California. This dish offers the satisfying crunch of fried calamari, with charred chiles, a sharp green-tomato-and-corn relish, and pickled red onions creating a cavalcade of color and contrast. The butter lettuce leaves create cups full of nooks and crannies to capture all the flavors.

SERVES 4

CORNMEAL-CRUSTED SQUID SALAD

LEMON POBLANO MAYO Preheat the broiler and set the oven rack to the topmost position. Line a baking sheet with aluminum foil, and set the poblano on the sheet. Broil, turning occasionally, until blackened on all sides. Remove from the oven and set aside until cool enough to handle. Peel off the skin, slice pepper open to remove the seeds, and coarsely chop.

In a food processor or blender (or using an immersion blender), combine the egg, egg yolk, lemon zest and juice, and salt and pepper. With the machine running, slowly add the oil in a thin steady stream. When the mixture is emulsified and thickened and all the oil has been incorporated, add the roasted peppers and puree until smooth. Stir in the lime zest and juice. Taste and adjust seasoning with more salt and pepper if desired. Refrigerate until ready to serve. Can be made ahead of time; will keep refrigerated for up to 3 days.

CORN AND GREEN TOMATO RELISH Combine all the ingredients in a bowl. Season to taste with sea salt. (Best served the same day it is made.)

SWEET AND SOUR RED ONIONS In a saucepan, combine the water, vinegar, sugar, and salt, and bring to a boil over medium-high heat, stirring until the salt and sugar dissolve. Place the onions in a nonreactive bowl, then pour the hot liquid over them. Set aside to cool. (Can be made several days ahead and refrigerated.)

SALAD Slice the tubes into rings and slice the tentacles in half. Combine the squid and buttermilk in a bowl and refrigerate overnight.

Drain the squid, discarding the buttermilk, and lightly pat dry (you want it to be a bit moist). Combine the cornstarch and cornmeal in a shallow bowl. Drop the squid in the mixture and toss to coat.

In a heavy-bottomed saucepan or Dutch oven, heat at least 2 inches of oil over medium-high heat until it reaches 375°F.

Working in batches to avoid overcrowding, deep-fry the squid in the hot oil for about 1 minute or until crispy. (It won't be browned, just crisp. You don't want to overcook the squid as it will become tough.) Using a slotted spoon, transfer the squid to a plate lined with paper towels to drain. Season with salt and chili powder.

To assemble, arrange the lettuce leaves on a platter. Drizzle with the mayonnaise, then add the relish and drained pickled onions. Top with the crispy squid. Serve with tortillas or corn chips.

LEMON POBLANO MAYO
1 fresh poblano chile pepper, stem removed
1 egg
1 egg yolk
Zest and juice of 1 lemon
½ tsp sea salt
½ tsp coarsely ground black pepper
1 cup canola oil
Zest and juice of 1 lime

CORN AND GREEN TOMATO RELISH
1 cup fresh corn kernels
2 green (unripe) tomatoes, diced
½ scallion, chopped
2 Tbsp extra-virgin olive oil
1 tsp sea salt

SWEET AND SOUR RED ONIONS
1½ cups water
1½ cups red wine vinegar
¼ cup granulated sugar
2 Tbsp sea salt
1 red onion, halved, core removed, and thinly sliced

SALAD
1 lb cleaned squid, tubes and tentacles
2 cups buttermilk
½ cup cornstarch, for dredging
½ cup cornmeal, for dredging
Canola oil, for deep-frying
Sea salt
Chili powder
1 head butter lettuce, leaves torn
Soft white corn tortillas or yellow corn chips, to serve

Squid can become tough and rubbery when cooked, so it needs to be either marinated (or tenderized) and flash-cooked or braised until meltingly tender. I've opted for the latter route in this ragout, with charred tomatoes, potatoes, and black beans. Slow-baking brings out all the rich flavors in the dish.

BLACK BEANS
1 cup dried black beans
   (see Notes)
3 cups cold water
1 bay leaf
½ onion, quartered
½ tsp sea salt

CHARRED TOMATOES
6 to 8 Roma tomatoes,
   halved
2 Tbsp olive oil
Sea salt and coarsely
   ground black pepper

SQUID RAGOUT
1 lb California Market squid,
   cleaned
2 to 3 lb Yukon gold
   potatoes, peeled and
   sliced into ¼-inch-thick
   disks
1 onion, thinly sliced
1 serrano chile, seeded and
   thinly sliced
1 tsp sea salt
½ cup olive oil
Zest and juice of 1 lemon
¼ cup chopped flat-leaf
   parsley, for garnish
Crusty bread, sliced, to
   serve
Garden salad, to serve

SERVES 4

SQUID RAGOUT

BLACK BEANS Preheat the oven to 325°F. Pick through the beans and discard any stones, debris, or shriveled beans. Rinse well, transfer to a large pot, and add the water, bay leaf, and onion. Cover and bring to a boil over high heat. Transfer to the oven and cook for 1 hour. Stir in the salt and continue cooking for another 30 minutes or until tender. Drain the beans. (Can be made and refrigerated several days ahead.)

CHARRED TOMATOES Preheat the broiler and set the oven rack about 4 inches below it (or preheat the grill to high heat). In a medium bowl, toss the tomatoes with olive oil, and season with salt and pepper. Arrange the tomatoes cut side down in an even layer on a rimmed baking sheet (or grill grate) and cook until charred, about 5 minutes. Turn over and cook the other side for another 3 minutes or until caramelized. Remove from the oven and roughly chop. Add the black beans and mix well.

SQUID RAGOUT Preheat the oven to 375°F. Using a mallet, pound the squid steaks gently and evenly on all sides to lightly tenderize. Cut into ½-inch-wide strips.

Line the bottom of a shallow baking dish with the sliced potatoes. Scatter over the onions and chile, add the salt, and pour in the olive oil. Bake for 20 minutes. Add the squid, black beans, and charred tomatoes, and cook for another 25 minutes or until the squid is tender.

Remove from the oven, add the lemon zest and juice, and garnish with parsley.

Serve with crusty bread and a side salad.

CHEF'S NOTES: You might be surprised to find I don't recommend soaking beans before cooking—unless they've been rattling around your pantry for a couple years. It turns out, soaking doesn't speed up the cooking process by any worthwhile degree unless your beans are very old. But most importantly, it waters down the beans' flavor. Try cooking them straight from their dried state, and see for yourself.

SEA GREENS

DULSE • 169

[profile 215]

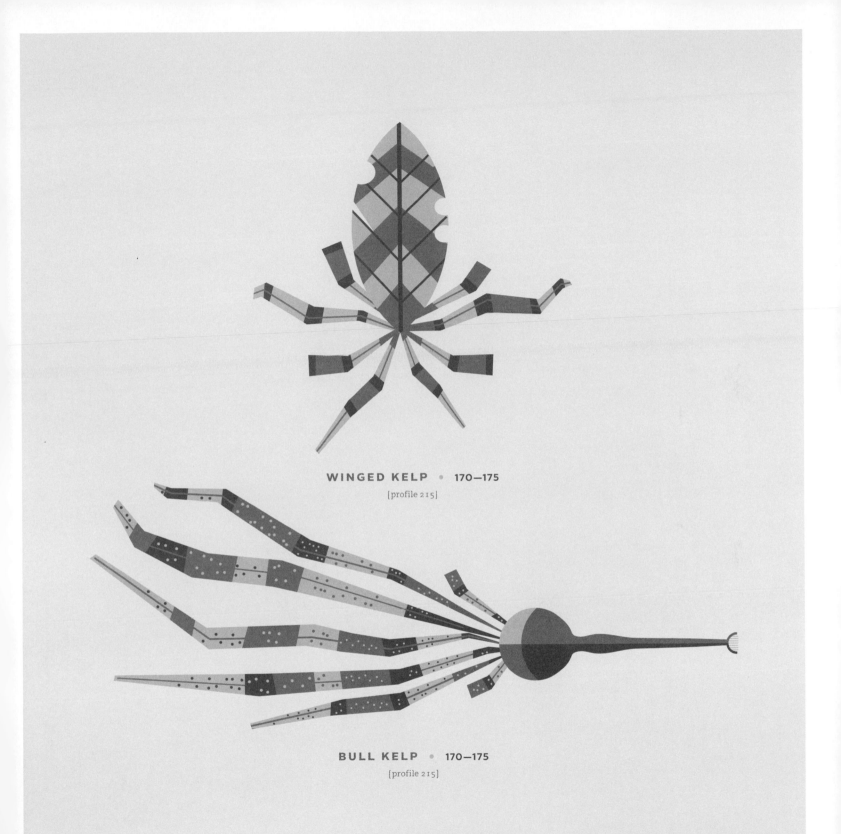

WINGED KELP • 170—175

[profile 215]

BULL KELP • 170—175

[profile 215]

SEA GREENS

SEAWEED IS SO VERSATILE and has one of the broadest ranges of minerals contained by any single ingredient on earth. Available both wild and farmed, there are a handful of edible seaweeds up and down the coast. North Americans have long overlooked edible ocean plants, while home cooks in places such as Japan, Ireland, and China have enthusiastically embraced them. They add wonderful salty and umami notes to dishes as varied as sushi, salad, and pudding.

I encourage you to get comfortable adding it to your own favorite dishes and reaping the health benefits. Chopped sea greens are delicious additions to soups or broths, and with notable emulsifying properties, they make for inventive custards, ice creams, and silky chocolate pudding. Kelp can lend savory notes and chewier texture when paired with spinach. It can be used in a compound butter that's exceptional slathered onto fish or shellfish for heightened ocean flavor.

Not sure where to get started in this chapter? I've never met a diner who didn't love my Kelp and Smoked Sea Salt Scones with Serrano Butter (page 172). These ocean-infused baked goods combine the element of surprise with the comfort factor. Warm from the oven and generously spread with hot and spicy butter, they make a delicious snack or accompaniment to chowder or seafood dips or broths.

You'll also find recipes calling for seaweed scattered throughout the book. Check out Raw Oysters with Pickled Seaweed (page 142); Mussels in Creamy, Spicy Seaweed Broth (page 131); and Sea Urchin Custard with Dulse and Sea Asparagus Salsa Verde (page 152). Once you've tried a few of these dishes, you might find yourself experimenting with sea greens in your own dinner repertoire for extra briny flavor—and all the nutritional rewards.

These cookies are perfect for refueling after a hike, run, or yoga class, to get your energy back up and accelerate muscle repair. I ate them as a daily treat on my Chefs for Oceans ride across Canada. Go to nextjen.ca for a list of stores that carry Nextjen's gluten-free flour mix. Another great gluten-free blend is Thomas Keller's Cup4Cup.

MAKES ABOUT
26 COOKIES

DULSE, DARK CHOCOLATE, AND CRANBERRY POWER COOKIES

Preheat oven to 300°F and line 3 baking sheets with parchment paper.

In a large bowl, combine the oats, flour, 4 kinds of seeds, coconut, seaweed, cinnamon, salt, chocolate chips, and cranberries and mix until well combined.

In another large bowl, whisk together the honey, water, soy milk, oil, and molasses. Pour this mixture over the dry ingredients and stir until everything is well combined. Place firmly packed ½-cup mounds of cookie dough onto prepared baking sheets. (I find the easiest way to portion cookie dough is with a large ice cream scoop.) Flatten cookies slightly, and bake for 16 minutes. Serve.

CHEF'S NOTES: Cookies are best warm—however, they do freeze well. After baking, transfer to a wire rack and allow to cool to room temperature before freezing. When ready to eat, thaw at room temperature and warm in the microwave for 30 seconds.

3 cups plus 2½ Tbsp old-fashioned (rolled) oats
3¼ cups Nextjen Gluten-Free All-Purpose Baking Blend (or your favorite gluten-free flour mix)
1½ cups sunflower seeds
1¼ cups pumpkin seeds
½ cup plus 2 Tbsp hemp seeds
⅓ cup flaxseeds
¾ cup unsweetened dried shredded coconut
1¾ cups finely dried seaweed such as finely chopped dulse or flaked kelp
1½ Tbsp ground cinnamon
2½ tsp sea salt
2½ cups organic dark chocolate chips
2½ cups dried cranberries
¾ cup honey
¼ cup plus 2 Tbsp water
1½ cups unsweetened soy milk
1 cup coconut or vegetable oil
¼ cup fancy molasses

The Caesar isn't just a salad. It's also Canada's beloved take on the Bloody Mary. What's the difference? The Caesar is always made with clam juice. I love preparing it with Walter Caesar Mix, made in small batches with all-natural ingredients. Of course, the best part about any Caesar (or Bloody Mary) is the garnishes. I always serve mine pimped out with all kinds of additions, plus a dozen shucked oysters on the side. Here I've kept things simple with fresh spot prawns for each serving, but feel free to skewer a few of your favorite garnishes, such as pickled green beans, olives, bacon, and of course crisp, peeled celery.

SERVES 4

CAESAR WITH SEAWEED VODKA "PRAWN COCKTAIL" AND SMOKED SEA SALT AND MAPLE RIM

RIM In a shallow bowl, combine the brown sugar, sea salt, and paprika. Pour the maple syrup into a separate shallow bowl. Dip the rim of 4 pint glasses in the maple syrup, and then into the sugar and salt mixture to coat.

COCKTAIL In a pitcher, mix together the Caesar mix (or Clamato or tomato juice and clam juice), horseradish, lemon zest and juice, Tabasco, Worcestershire, and pepper. Taste and adjust seasonings if desired.

Fill each glass with ice. Divide the cocktail mix among the glasses, then top each with 2 ounces of vodka. Hook 2 to 3 spot prawns onto the side of each glass, garnish with a slice of kelp and lemon, and sprinkle the flaked kelp on top. Serve.

CHEF'S NOTES: Although plain vodka works perfectly well, you can add a dimension of flavor with seaweed-infused vodka. Simply combine a 4-inch piece of kombu (i.e., dried kelp), or your favorite fresh or pickled seaweed, in 1 cup of vodka. Allow to infuse overnight, then strain and use.

To poach spot prawns, bring a small pot of salted water or broth to a boil. Place the unpeeled prawns (fresh or thawed) in a bowl and pour the boiling water or broth over them. Allow to sit for 30 seconds. Remove with a slotted spoon and transfer to an ice-water bath to cool. Drain, peel, and refrigerate until ready to serve.

RIM

¼ cup packed light brown sugar

¼ cup smoked sea salt (see Notes on page 146); I prefer Vancouver Island Sea Salt)

1 Tbsp smoked paprika

⅓ cup pure maple syrup

COCKTAIL

7 cups Walter Caesar Mix or Clamato, or 5 cups tomato juice and 2 cups clam juice

1 Tbsp plus 1 tsp prepared horseradish

Zest and juice of 2 lemons

4 dashes of Tabasco sauce

4 dashes of Worcestershire sauce

Coarsely ground black pepper

8 fl oz (1 cup) seaweed vodka (see Notes)

12 poached spot prawns, heads removed, for garnish (see Notes)

1 Tbsp flaked dried bull kelp, for garnish

4 strips hydrated bull or winged kelp, for garnish

4 lemon slices, for garnish

Admittedly, seaweed scones sound like something a mermaid would eat, but bear with me: these salty, savory biscuits are a game changer. Fresh out of the oven and spread with melting spicy butter, they're unbeatable with a bowl of chunky chowder or a citrus-dressed seafood salad. The unbaked scones freeze well, which means you can keep some in the freezer to bake whenever the mood strikes.

SERRANO BUTTER

2 serrano or jalapeño
   peppers, stems removed
1 cup (2 sticks) unsalted
   butter, softened
1 Tbsp honey
1½ tsp sea salt

KELP SCONES

3 cups all-purpose flour,
   plus extra for dusting
2 Tbsp granulated sugar
1 Tbsp plus 2 tsp baking
   powder
1 Tbsp smoked sea salt
   (see Notes on page 146)
2 Tbsp kelp powder
   (see Notes)
Zest of ½ lemon
¾ cup (1½ sticks) cold
   unsalted butter, cut into
   ½-inch cubes
1 cup whole milk
1 egg

MAKES 8

KELP AND SMOKED SEA SALT SCONES

SERRANO BUTTER Preheat the broiler and set the oven rack to the topmost position. Put the peppers on a baking sheet and broil on one side for about 5 minutes or until beginning to soften and the skins are browned or blackened. Use tongs to turn the peppers over and broil for another 5 minutes or until browned. Set aside to cool.

When cool enough to handle, scrape off the skins. Split the peppers open and remove the seeds. Transfer the peppers to a blender or food processor, add the butter, honey, and salt, and process until well blended. Scrape the butter onto a piece of plastic wrap, and then shape and roll it into a 2-inch-thick log. Refrigerate until needed.

KELP SCONES Preheat the oven to 400°F. Line a baking sheet with parchment paper.

In the bowl of a food processor, pulse the flour, sugar, baking powder, smoked salt, kelp powder, and lemon zest until combined. Add the butter and pulse until the mixture resembles coarse cornmeal scattered with a few larger pea-size pieces of butter. (Alternatively, you can use a stand mixer, or cut the butter in by hand with a pastry cutter.)

In a separate bowl, whisk together the milk and egg until well combined. Add to the flour mixture and pulse just a few times until the dough starts to come together. Do not overmix. Turn the dough out onto a clean, dry work surface. Gather and press it together to form a cohesive ball.

Sprinkle the work surface lightly with flour. Roll or pat the dough into a 1-inch-thick circle. Use a sharp knife to cut the dough into 8 wedges. Arrange the scones on the prepared baking sheet, spacing them about 1 inch apart. Bake for 15 minutes or until golden brown. Serve warm with the serrano butter.

CHEF'S NOTES: Kelp powder is available at many well-stocked supermarkets in the nutritional supplements aisle or through farmers' markets and online retailers.

To make the scones from frozen, just reduce the heat to 375°F and bake about 10 minutes longer.

With two nutrient-dense star ingredients—dark chocolate and kelp—these fudgy brownies slathered in chocolate icing could almost be considered a health food. The inspiration for the sole dessert in this book comes from my love of salted caramel—not from my misspent youth, I swear! Kelp has a delicate saltiness that opens the taste buds and enhances the rich and sweet flavors of this special brownie—no hallucinogens required.

MAKES 2 DOZEN

(SEA)WEED BROWNIES

BROWNIES Preheat the oven to 325°F. Line a rimmed baking sheet (12 × 18 × 2 inches) with parchment paper.

Melt the butter and chocolate in a heatproof bowl set over a pot of simmering water. Stir until melted. Remove the bowl from the heat and allow to cool slightly.

In a large bowl, whisk together the granulated sugar, brown sugar, eggs, and vanilla. Stir in the cooled chocolate mixture.

Sift the flour and cocoa powder together over the chocolate mixture and stir until incorporated. Stir in the kelp powder (or flaked seaweed) and sea salt.

Pour the batter into the prepared baking sheet and bake for 30 minutes. Set aside to cool.

FROSTING Combine all the ingredients in the bowl of a stand mixer fitted with the whisk attachment (or use a handheld mixer), and whip until smooth and creamy.

When the brownies have cooled, spread the frosting on top and garnish with kelp powder (or flaked seaweed). They're at their best warm, so don't hesitate to throw them in the microwave for 30 seconds before serving.

BROWNIES

1½ cups (3 sticks) unsalted butter
6 oz chopped high-quality dark chocolate, such as Cacao Barry, Valrhona, or Scharffen Berger
1¼ cups granulated sugar
1½ cups packed brown sugar
6 eggs
1 Tbsp vanilla paste or vanilla extract
1⅔ cups all-purpose flour
1⅔ cups cocoa powder (preferably Dutch-process)
1 oz (about ¼ cup) kelp powder or flaked seaweed, plus extra for garnish
1 Tbsp sea salt

FROSTING

1 cup (2 sticks) unsalted butter, softened
1 cup cocoa powder
½ cup honey
1 Tbsp vanilla paste or vanilla extract
1 tsp sea salt
5 cups confectioners' sugar, sifted

SPECIES PROFILES

As **founder of** Chefs for Oceans and executive chef of Ocean Wise, I'm committed to raising awareness around sustainable seafood. Over the years, I've been fortunate enough to meet with some of our oceans' most respected leaders and advocates. The most responsible decisions are made when we commit to keeping informed about the research around our ocean habitats. I support consuming the species in this book (in moderation), based on the most up-to-date studies available at this time.

A good start on your journey to eating more ocean-friendly fish and shellfish is to get familiar with the five sustainable species of wild Pacific salmon: sockeye, pink, chum, coho, and spring. Pink is the smallest and leanest and also the most sustainable. Sockeye is coveted among chefs for its darker flesh. Spring—also known as king or Chinook—is by far my favorite: it is the largest and just so full of rich flavor. Coho and chum are the workhorse species—softer fleshed and perfect for bouillabaisse (page 81) and paella (page 90). And let's not forget there are also some salmon farms getting it right today with land-based recirculating systems. Kuterra salmon is a beautiful-tasting, firm-fleshed option from BC.

Another simple shift you can make to introduce more sustainable fatty fish into your repertoire is to switch out challenged big red tunas for more abundant Pacific albacore tuna. It's less dark and steaky but, in my opinion, more flavorful. And albacore tuna is caught by pole or troll, which creates minimal bycatch.

Also, develop a taste for smaller species such as silvery sardines and mackerel. These are lower in mercury—a concern with larger oily fish—and they reach maturity faster. They can be sustainably caught using the purse seine method, which leaves the seabed intact.

And when it comes to sustainability, shellfish are right up there. Shellfish can be divided into two categories: mollusks and crustaceans. Mollusks such as clams, mussels, and oysters draw nutrients from the algae in their natural environment. As natural filter feeders, they actually leave the ocean cleaner.

Most Pacific mollusks such as clams, mussels, and oysters are farmed. Bag-and-rack culture involves raising juveniles in bags stretched across racks just above the seabed. Farmers often grow these shellfish on ropes, mesh bags, and what look like extralong socks, suspended from colorful buoys bobbing on the surface of the water. The impact on surrounding sea life is minimal.

There are no Pacific fisheries for octopus or squid. Often when fishers are out to catch a different species, they'll bring an octopus up onto the boat stuck to a long line or inside a trap. Instead of throwing it back and having it potentially die, they are allowed to keep it to sell as food. Spiny-shelled sea urchins—which are prized for their roe—are typically hand-harvested by divers from the ocean floor, again creating zero bycatch.

To harvest wild crustaceans—shrimp, crabs, and lobsters—responsible fishers use traps or pots. They lower them to the ocean floor with tasty bait inside so that the creatures wander in and become trapped inside.

But what few people realize is that the most nutrient-dense food source from the ocean with the most potential to feed the planet is actually seaweed. When I was a child, I perceived seaweed to be a fun toy for whipping my friends on the beach and a tickly inconvenience on ocean swims. These days, as a long-distance runner and cyclist, I view it as one of the most nutritious sources of fuel for my body. And as an environmentalist, I believe it's the plant that might just save the world.

Sea greens—or algae—grow in all the shades you'd see in a healthy autumnal forest: greens, reds, purples, ochers, and yellows. Under the sea, the colors often take on more vibrancy, which makes them all the more attractive as they gently dance and sway with the movements of the tides. From fan-shaped winged kelp to crimp-edged dulse, these wild plants exhibit an astonishing array of forms and textures. North Americans have long overlooked edible ocean plants, while home cooks in places such as Japan, Ireland, and China have enthusiastically embraced them. They add wonderful salty and umami notes to dishes as varied as sushi, salad, and pudding.

What excites me most about sea greens is their ocean-purifying powers. They can convert the nitrogen in polluted marine waters into healthy living tissue, effectively reviving dead zones. Since seaweed thrives in the same places as shellfish, many oyster and mussel farmers are now growing and harvesting both in balanced ecosystems that leave the environment cleaner.

If you're lucky enough to live on the coast, you should be able to connect with a fishmonger or sea green forager to get whatever is fresh and in season. More and more fish vendors are stocking sea greens harvested by their shellfish suppliers—just ask.

CHAR

RECIPES *pages 39 to 41*

• • • A FISH TALE • • •

I first saw a char fish farm in the last place you'd expect it: in the Okanagan Valley surrounded by vineyards and fruit trees. Gary Klassen's land-based business DelicaSea sits in the heart of BC wine country, overlooking the desert region of Osoyoos. When I stopped by on the final stretch of my Chefs for Oceans ride, I was grateful for the chance to stretch my legs and check out this Ocean Wise–approved oasis.

• • • A SUSTAINABILITY STORY • • •

While Gary is raising hatchlings from the Arctic, so technically not a Pacific species, I've included his farmed char in this book because he's operating on the West Coast, using best practices in sustainable aquaculture. The relatively small wild-char fishery in Nunavut would never be able to serve all of North America itself. By 2050, our global population is expected to rise from over seven billion to nine billion, so responsible fish farming is one means of ensuring there's enough healthy protein for all.

The flow-through recirculating aquaculture system at DelicaSea draws fresh water from an 80-feet-deep aquifer at a brisk 12°C (54°F), re-creating the conditions of the char's natural habit in glacier-fed lakes and arctic and subarctic coastal waters. Any waste is converted into fertilizer, to enrich the soils of nearby wineries and orchards.

• • • CATCH OF THE DAY • • •

A striking fish, char changes from a greenish-brown color with a pale pink belly and pink spots to a deep red during spawning. My go-to in winter, when wild salmon season is over, this fish is rich, dense, and luxuriously fatty. Tastewise it sits on the spectrum between salmon and lake trout: its rosy flesh has a clean, neutral flavor and surprisingly delicate texture. Char is beautiful baked, pan-seared, or roasted, and with all its natural oils, almost impossible to overcook. The skin is papery thin and crisps to perfection. A substantial fish, it lends itself well to cold-season complements such as rustic lentils and root vegetables (page 41), and luxuriously rich brown butter and birch syrup with comforting whole grains (page 39).

• • • PREP IT LIKE YOU OWN IT • • •

To infuse char with flavor, poach it in a court bouillon of chopped shallots or onions, celery, and fennel, with white wine, peppercorns, and a bay leaf.

Littleneck

Manila

Savory/
Purple varnish

Butter

LITTLENECK
Protothaca staminea

MANILA
Venerupis philippinarum

BUTTER
Saxidomus gigantea

SAVORY/PURPLE VARNISH
Nuttallia obscurata

●

CLAMS

RECIPES *pages 109 to 115*

• • • A FISH TALE • • •

I often take my sons to Asian wet markets, where butchered meat and live or prepared fresh fish and shellfish are sold. They peer, fascinated, into the seafood tanks full of interesting fish, bivalves, and crustaceans, and they watch the vendors deftly shuck, debone, or declaw creatures that were in motion moments before.

We North Americans are accustomed to seeing sea creatures canned or neatly packaged on Styrofoam trays, so it can be jarring to observe them moving around in their live state. But we develop more respect for fish and shellfish when we acknowledge they've given their lives, and when we buy the freshest possible products, we experience seafood at its most vibrant and flavorful.

• • • A SUSTAINABILITY STORY • • •

As filter feeders, clams absorb their nutrients from the water, leaving it cleaner. In the U.S. and Canada, tight regulations protect coastal areas where clams are farmed since these creatures are extravulnerable to pollution.

• • • CATCH OF THE DAY • • •

The flavor and textural differences between the Pacific clam species are subtle enough that I just use the freshest available, whatever dish I'm making. There are a few distinguishing qualities nonetheless: littleneck clams, not surprisingly, have tiny necks; one of the smallest Pacific clams, they have the brightest and briniest flavors. Manilas are soft and sweet, with a decent-size piece of flesh. Also known as purple varnish or purple mahogany clams, savory clams have glossy shell interiors, ranging from pale violet to deep purple. Their flesh is delicate, sweet, and a little chewy. And butter clams have crunchy texture.

Clams are one of the most affordable things we can make for family and friends. They're incredibly easy to prepare, whether served in their shells combined with golden baked potatoes with horseradish and lemon (page 110), or steamed in craft beer with leeks and butter (page 111). You can start with beer, wine, stock, or juice and then add aromatics like thyme, shallots, or garlic for a comforting broth- or sauce-based dish.

• • • PREP IT LIKE YOU OWN IT • • •

There's no need to soak store-bought clams in salt water as they will have been purged of sand. Transfer them to a bowl and loosely cover them with a damp towel, and store them in the coolest part of your fridge. Don't clean them until you're ready to cook them. Rinse clams vigorously with cold running water for a good five minutes. If a clam's shells are agape, tap the creature a few times and they should close up. If they don't, then discard the clam.

COD

RECIPES *pages 43 to 45*

• • • A FISH TALE • • •

My middle son, Max, loves going for fish and chips with Daddy. Our favorite Vancouver spot is the Fish Counter, co-owned by my sustainable seafood heroes Chef Rob Clark and marine biologist Mike McDermid, who cofounded the Ocean Wise sustainable seafood program. Max always goes for the Pacific cod—a tender and flaky fish—but I suspect it was the salty, mayonnaise-y aspect of it that first reeled him in.

• • • A SUSTAINABILITY STORY • • •

While the bulk of Pacific cod comes from Northern BC and Alaska, it is also caught in California, Oregon, and Washington. Most Pacific cod on the West Coast is now considered sustainable. I like to choose midwater trawled because the nets don't touch the ocean floor. And longlines, pots, and jigs leave the marine environment intact and create next to no bycatch.

• • • CATCH OF THE DAY • • •

Tender and flaky with near translucent flesh, Pacific cod is a smaller fish than Atlantic cod, with more manageably sized loins. It lends itself well to more delicate cooking methods, such as steaming or cooking *en papillote*. Never smother this fish in heavy sauces or drown it out with pungent spices and powerful flavors. It will shine with lighter elements, such as citrus, melting butter, spring peas, and fluffy mashed potatoes. Some green for contrast never goes amiss, which is why the fish tastes and looks so good on the plate with a trio of broccoli preparations (page 44).

• • • PREP IT LIKE YOU OWN IT • • •

Pacific cod is a delicate fish that needs to be flash frozen on the boat or eaten fresh within 48 hours of harvest. You don't need to batter and deep-fry it, and in fact you'll get to appreciate its subtle flavor if you don't. The trick to perfectly cooked cod is a hot pan, hot oil, and clean and dry fish. Let the pan do its job to get that gorgeous caramelized crust.

Snow

King

Dungeness

DUNGENESS
Metacarcinus magister

KING
Paralithodes camtschaticus

SNOW
Chionoecetes opilio

CRAB

RECIPES *pages 116 to 125*

• • • A FISH TALE • • •

One of the most creative dishes I've ever tasted was snow crab Scotch eggs made by John Higgins, the George Brown College Chef School director and *Chopped Canada* judge who started out at Buckingham Palace. Ethereal snow crab and warm-yolked eggs were just meant to be together.

• • • A SUSTAINABILITY STORY • • •

Crab fishers harvest with traps or pots, which creates minimal bycatch and damage to the marine environment. Some of my recipes call for Dungeness crab, which is abundant and readily available in most Pacific regions. Dungeness fisheries are managed by trap size, crab size and sex, and season (only large males are harvested so the females can reproduce). The rest of my recipes call for either king crab or snow crab, which both live longer and reproduce less but have exceptionally well-managed fisheries on the Pacific coast.

• • • CATCH OF THE DAY • • •

Dungeness crab is worth the splurge for its sweet and tender flesh. I like it as a decadent topping to mac 'n' cheese (page 122). King crab is a huge long-legged beast whose rich and nutty flesh is luscious in an updated Cobb salad (page 120). And snow crab is prized for its delicate and sweet meat; it shines in the crab cakes (page 116).

• • • PREP IT LIKE YOU OWN IT • • •

Ask your fishmonger to kill fresh crab for you or get it straight home and steam it, 6 minutes per pound. (King crab is already cooked and frozen in the harbor so only needs to be steamed for 5 minutes to reheat.) Crack open harder shells with pliers or heavy-duty shellfish crackers—avoid mallets as they break up the meat. With kitchen shears, snip open the legs so you can gently pull or pick out the flesh. The main shell contains a little flesh worth extracting too. Discard the pale-greenish innards (tomalley) inside the main shell, picking off larger pieces with your fingers, and running fresh cold water over what's left. Do save all the shells and juices—they make flavorful stock.

GEODUCK

RECIPE *page 126 to 127*

• • • A FISH TALE • • •

I had the chance to cook for Prince William and Kate at Mission Hill Winery in BC. They sampled a variety of sustainable seafood dishes, but the British and North American media fixated on the geoduck, which the prince diplomatically described as "presentationally challenging." When you break this giant clam down, you get the meat, the shell, and a large neck-like tube called the siphon, which can grow up to a yard long. It can be a little intimidating—and the butt of risqué jokes—because of its appearance.

• • • A SUSTAINABILITY STORY • • •

These burrowing creatures feed on plankton, leaving the marine environment cleaner. On the Pacific coast, geoduck is harvested in remote areas—in carefully managed wild and cultivated fisheries—by skillful divers 15 to 60 feet beneath the surface of the water down on the sandy ocean floor. Each geoduck is handpicked, so bycatch and environmental damage are virtually zero.

• • • CATCH OF THE DAY • • •

These days we treat geoduck as a delicacy, but you could once barely give away this shellfish. Geoduck's body meat is pleasingly fleshy, and its neck meat has a firm texture and something of a snap. This shellfish used to be the main ingredient in BC Ferries' clam chowder. Japanese chefs use it for sushi and sashimi; you can spot it on their menus under the name *mirugai*. And in Chinese restaurants, you'll often see it in the live tanks before it ends up the centerpiece of a showy platter. I like to take this strange ingredient and put it into a familiar dish, such as nachos, with a bright and creamy avocado and grapefruit vinaigrette (page 126), or a warming tomato chowder (page 114), to eliminate the fear factor.

• • • PREP IT LIKE YOU OWN IT • • •

To remove a geoduck's shell, slide in a butter knife (it doesn't even need to be sharp) and gently disengage the body. Next, cut away the meat, and separate the siphon from the body meat. Dunk the siphon in boiling water, then into an ice bath, to remove its sheath. Then slice the siphon down the middle and cut it crosswise into thin slices. The body meat can be thinly sliced and sautéed in butter for a few seconds. Cube it and it will make a great addition for a clam chowder.

HALIBUT

RECIPES *pages 46 to 53*

• • • A FISH TALE • • •

My halibut fisher Wes Erickson is a fisherman *and* a chef. After a fishing trip, he'll sometimes forage for seaweed and shellfish to throw in the pot, and then cook them up alongside his halibut catch. This species is the world's largest flatfish and can reach over six hundred pounds and almost 10 feet. Wes talks to me about his experiences at sea because he knows how important storytelling is to chefs when we're coaxing diners into trying something new. I have huge respect for men and women like him who go out in the middle of nowhere—sometimes in the middle of the night—and pull up their catch in all weathers, literally risking their lives to offer us this last source of wild protein.

• • • A SUSTAINABILITY STORY • • •

Pacific halibut live up to 42 years old and mature slowly, yet they're considered sustainable because their fisheries are so well managed with scientifically determined catch limits, individual quotas, research surveys, stock assessments to track population, and rigorous at-sea and dockside monitoring of catch.

• • • CATCH OF THE DAY • • •

Dense and flavorful, halibut has four boneless fillets: two darker-fleshed ones on top and two pearly-white ones on the bottom.

This coloring evolved as a camouflage, to make the flatfish barely visible to predators as it skims the ocean floor. Any halibut above 80 pounds will have fillets too thick and unwieldy to cook whole. But don't worry, the product at your local fishmonger will be around 30 pounds. The heads are chopped off on the boat, but I ask my suppliers to save the cheeks—with their silky, scallop-like texture, they're a delicacy.

Because it's so lean, halibut soaks up the flavor from marinades. Although it grills well, baking dries it out. A moist-heat method—such as pan-searing, poaching, or steaming—is best. Try halibut with spring peas and spinach (page 49) or with spicy clam broth (page 52). This fish has the structure to make a fine burger, so be sure to try my signature halibut burger with BC blueberries (page 46).

• • • PREP IT LIKE YOU OWN IT • • •

Make marinade with a 2-to-1 ratio of olive oil to acid (citrus juice), chopped shallots, and slices of lemon or lime zest. Add stems of herbs that you've bruised to awaken their flavors, then remove these before cooking the fish. Don't marinate Pacific halibut for more than 15 to 20 minutes—any longer and it will cook in the acids.

LINGCOD

RECIPES *pages 53 to 56*

• • • A FISH TALE • • •

Lingcod has a potbelly, Shrek-like head, and the kind of sharp, gnarly teeth that children draw on monsters. Mottled with all kinds of browns, grays, greens, and yellows, it actually looks like it's dressed in leopard-skin print. This fish is the aging rocker of the deep, and I'm a die-hard fan.

• • • A SUSTAINABILITY STORY • • •

Lingcod is caught as part of a well-regulated multispecies fishery of groundfish. Various harvesting methods are deemed sustainable, but troll—or pole-and-line—is best because the fishers catch just one fish at a time and can release those that don't meet size requirements, as well as any other species that accidentally gets hooked. Most harvesting methods, including trawl, are now considered sustainable thanks to improvements in catch monitoring, reduction of habitat impacts, and incentives to use selective measures to reduce bycatch. I like the troll method best.

• • • CATCH OF THE DAY • • •

Related neither to ling nor cod, lingcod was so-named because it has a similar taste profile to both. This fish tastes fairly neutral, like cod, and has the silkiness of ling. A relatively lean fish, it lends itself well to big, bold, and rich complements. Lingcod's long, stringy, and luxurious cheeks—almost like rabbit rillettes—are a fisherman's prize. They don't fetch enough money to sell, but they're the best part.

Wildly underrated, lingcod is a workhorse. In spite of its flaky texture, it can stand up to battering and deep-frying. You can also pan-fry it in butter for lobster-like results. It responds well to grilling, baking, or roasting. Green-tinged in its natural state, the flesh turns white through cooking. I like to play with this palette, seeking out ingredients in similar hues, such as cabbage (page 56) to serve with the fish.

• • • PREP IT LIKE YOU OWN IT • • •

To prepare lingcod for grilling, baking, or roasting, just pat it dry with paper towel—skin on or skin off—for optimum caramelization. Brush it with olive oil, then season with salt and pepper. If you didn't buy the fish deboned, remove the line of bones running down the center of the loins using a fish boning knife. Run it down either side of the center line of bones, cutting all the way through the skin, removing the bones down the middle of the fillet.

MUSSELS

RECIPES *pages 129 to 135*

• • • A FISH TALE • • •

My parents loved mussels and would often cook us up a big pot when I was a child. We'd all sit unusually quiet 'round the table, prying out the jiggly orange flesh with our forks and leaving an impressive tower of blue-black shells in our wake. Then came the best part: mopping up the rich and briny broth with hunks of crusty white bread. It's an inexpensive way to feed a family or a crowd—and it's downright delicious.

• • • A SUSTAINABILITY STORY • • •

Mussels are farmed in protected coves and cultivated on ropes, floating rafts, and nets. As filter feeders, these bivalves will leave the ocean cleaner than they found it. The first mussels I used as a chef were Saltspring Island Mussels (saltspringislandmussels.com). They're grown in BC and comprise both Atlantic blue and Gallo species—as well as a hybrid of the two—which ensures that the company can provide mussels that are fresh and in season year round.

• • • CATCH OF THE DAY • • •

Mussels are incredibly versatile. They can be steamed with white wine, beer, or even apple juice (page 130) and served on the table in five minutes, after coming home from work or school. I love them with the smoldering combination of oranges, olives, and smoked paprika in a salad (page 129). The Belgians, of course, have perfected their mussels by serving them with french fries, aioli, and ice-cold beer. But my favorite preparation is family style in a hearty stew or broth. I sometimes add seaweed for extra umami flavor (page 131) or serve them with a rich and comforting side of garlic confit, caramelized onions, and olive toast (page 135).

• • • PREP IT LIKE YOU OWN IT • • •

Most farm-raised mussels are grown on vertical rope farms and held in tanks before they're packaged and shipped to markets, so they should be fairly clean by the time they enter your kitchen. Transfer them to a bowl and loosely cover them with a damp towel, and store them in the coolest part of your fridge. Don't clean them until you're ready to cook them. Transfer the mussels to a colander and run them under cold water, rinsing away any debris or seaweed clinging to their shell. Remove the beard. If a mussel's shells are agape, tap the creature a few times and they should close up. If they don't, then discard the mussel.

OCTOPUS

RECIPES *pages 138 to 141*

• • • A FISH TALE • • •

When you bring an octopus onto the boat, you have to be careful: it is the world's greatest escape artist. In a laboratory setting, scientists have shown it's clever enough to solve puzzles, and with its boneless body, six arms, and two legs, this contortionist can get into more trouble than most other sea creatures by prizing open containers and jars and slipping through tiny gaps. My prawn and crab fisher Stewart McDonald will buzz me if an octopus comes up in his traps to ask if I want it. That is one of my favorite texts to receive. Since there's no targeted Pacific octopus fishery, these creatures are gold to chefs.

• • • A SUSTAINABILITY STORY • • •

Fishers harvesting cod, spot prawns, or Dungeness crab in traps or pots in the chillier waters of BC and Alaska are allowed to keep any Pacific Giant octopus brought up incidentally. While work needs to be done on tracking their population in both regions, fishers are limited to the number of Pacific Giant octopuses that can be claimed as bycatch in Alaska. The gears used—traps and pots—are kind to the environment.

• • • CATCH OF THE DAY • • •

Octopus has dense flesh, but its suckered tentacles become more tender when it's stewed in broth over low heat. I also love it brined and then grilled and served with a rich Mediterranean dipping sauce of roasted red peppers and almonds (page 138). To encourage people to expand their horizons, I'll team lesser-known species with something everybody loves. An offering such as seared scallops wrapped in cured, brined, and smoked octopus bacon (page 140) might give people the green light to try something initially intimidating, without committing to it as a solo-fish dish.

• • • PREP IT LIKE YOU OWN IT • • •

I suggest buying a pound or two frozen—just the limbs—so you don't have to tackle a huge whole octopus in your home kitchen. Freezing and then defrosting this creature actually helps break down its flesh and gives more tender results. Another benefit of frozen octopus is that it is already cleaned. Brine Pacific Giant octopus in a solution of 1 cup kosher salt, 1 cup granulated sugar, and 5 quarts water with aromatics such as bay leaves and peppercorns for at least 12 hours in the fridge.

OYSTERS

RECIPES *pages 142 to 146*

• • • A FISH TALE • • •

Last time I was at the Progress in San Francisco, Chef Stuart Brioza prepared an oyster dish for me that was a revelation. He served Hog Island Sweetwater oysters raw and topped with pickled Mendocino nori—a seaweed often sold in dried sheets for sushi, only here it was in fresh leafy strands. Near-translucent and vegetal, the nori created the perfect contrast in flavor and texture to the sweet and sour creamy-fleshed oysters. The whole dish was so well balanced, and the oyster practically melted in my mouth.

• • • A SUSTAINABILITY STORY • • •

We used to have abundant wild (Olympia) oysters on the West Coast—they were an important part of the First Nations peoples' diet. But the gold rush in the early 1900s led to pollution, habitat destruction, and over-fishing, which almost wiped out these creatures. The Pacific oyster seed (larvae) farmed on the North American Pacific coast was brought over from Japan between 1913 and WWII after the collapse of indigenous oyster stocks.

• • • CATCH OF THE DAY • • •

Compared to the brinier and more translucent-fleshed little Malpeques from the East Coast, Pacific oysters are meaty, dense, and creamy. The best way to eat them is with a squeeze of lemon for brightness and a tiny heap of fresh horseradish for bite. (What can I say? I'm a traditionalist.) Baking them really draws out their flavor, too—try them with a subtly sweet maple béarnaise sauce (page 145). And grilled with a craft beer, smoked salt, and honey butter (page 146), they make a bold appetizer.

• • • PREP IT LIKE YOU OWN IT • • •

Some people feel intimidated by an oyster's gnarly hard shell. Cracking it open doesn't require brute force; the trick is to find the perfect angle to slip the oyster knife right into the hinge. Wearing heavy gloves, partially wrap the oyster in a kitchen towel, then hold it down with one hand, cup side down. Insert an oyster knife (or any heavy-blade knife) into the hinge, and pry it open by twisting the knife to separate the top and bottom shells until the hinge pops.

ROCKFISH

RECIPES *pages 57 to 60*

• • • A FISH TALE • • •

Rockfish are everywhere: they swim low and high, and they hide out among the crevices in rocks under the sea. My home base Vancouver Aquarium offers identification classes so that divers and amateur fishers can tune in better to what they're seeing. The aquarium also invites divers once a year to submit videos from their dives so that marine biologists can use them to survey rockfish populations. The more we educate ourselves and work together, the better we can protect these and other fish.

• • • A SUSTAINABILITY STORY • • •

Rockfish is often misidentified as red snapper on menus. It's hard to make sustainable choices when you're being misled. Buying the fish whole, with its head, helps you to better identify it.

• • • CATCH OF THE DAY • • •

There are more than 70 species of rockfish in the Pacific, from California to Alaska. The canary (see left) are midwater trawled and deemed one of the more sustainable species. They have a bright-orange mottled body, a white stripe down the side, and if they're relatively young, black spots on the back. Quillbacks, also sustainable, have yellow markings—especially on the face—and a brownish body and spines down their back.

Lean, light, and flaky, rockfish are firm enough to retain their structure but still pleasantly delicate. They're relatively bony, but if you cook them whole (page 58), the bones come out a little easier and the results are moist. There are so many nooks and crannies in any rockfish for the juices, flavorings, and any finely chopped ingredients to collect. Rockfish has a nuttiness that works well with the deep, rich sweetness of roasted fruits (page 57). They also love a punchy mayo and the tang of pickles (page 60).

• • • PREP IT LIKE YOU OWN IT • • •

Rockfish is exceptionally flaky when cooked from its fresh state, but it perishes quickly, so you often see it frozen and turned into fish sticks or fish cakes. If you buy it live in a wet market, ask them to kill it for you, then cook it as quickly as possible afterward, when you get home. Otherwise, go for frozen and thaw it in the fridge. The slower you thaw the fish, the better it keeps its texture.

●

SABLEFISH

RECIPES *pages 71 to 74*

· · · A FISH TALE · · ·

About 20 years ago, sablefish went from under-the-radar species to the darling of chefs—it just tastes so luxurious with all its natural oils. Chef Hidekazu Tojo, of Vancouver restaurant Tojo's, brought the species into the limelight in Vancouver with his take on Nobu's miso-glazed sablefish. Versions of this dish appear in many West Coast restaurants now, but at the time, when he prepared it in his soulful little restaurant, many of us were tasting the species—as well as the bold sweet-salty-savory Asian-inspired flavor combination—for the first time.

· · · A SUSTAINABILITY STORY · · ·

Sablefish can live up to 90 years, lurking as deep as five thousand feet. In British Columbia, this slick, black bottom feeder is part of an integrated multispecies fishery, which includes dogfish and various species of rockfish, flatfish, and cod. The approach of harvesting more than one type of fish at a time is far more sustainable since it minimizes bycatch and makes fishers accountable for every fish they catch.

· · · CATCH OF THE DAY · · ·

Although not a member of the cod family, this gorgeous charcoal-skinned fish was previously known as black cod. It was rebranded as sablefish to sound sexier. Most of my sablefish dishes are big and bold. I'm partial to smoking this fish to give it bolder flavors and a little more structure, as in my brandade (page 74) and chowder (page 71) recipes. I also like using sweet-tart cranberries to balance the richness of sablefish (page 73).

· · · PREP IT LIKE YOU OWN IT · · ·

If you really want to barbecue this fatty fish, you'll need a grill pan so it doesn't flare up and scorch. For the best results, heat a cast-iron or stainless-steel grill pan over medium-high heat, slather the fish with canola oil and generous seasonings, and pan-sear for 3 to 4 minutes or until the fish forms a gorgeous crust with golden-brown caramelized edges.

Sockeye

Pink

Chinook

CHINOOK/SPRING
Oncorhynchus tshawytscha
CHUM
Oncorhynchus keta

COHO
Oncorhynchus kisutch
PINK
Oncorhynchus gorbuscha
SOCKEYE
Oncorhynchus nerka

STEELHEAD
Oncorhynchus mykiss
KUTERRA
Salmo salar

●

SALMON

RECITES *pages 75 to 96*

• • • A FISH TALE • • •

For millennia, the First Nations people on the West Coast have revered this species. They call it "the Giver of Life," recognizing that a healthy salmon run is crucial to so many other living things: eagles, bears, orcas, and even trees (eagles dive into the ocean for salmon, and they fly into the forest with their remains and fuel the ground where the trees grow).

And on the Northwest Pacific coast, there's a myth that salmon are actually immortal humans who live in the ocean, only coming up in springtime to feed hungry people. They say that throwing the salmon skeletons back into the river or ocean allows them to return to their underwater resting place and wait for the following spring so they can rise again as salmon people.

• • • A SUSTAINABILITY STORY • • •

To me, salmon is a magical fish. Four years after salmon are born, they know exactly where to travel to lay their eggs. They swim upstream from the ocean to their birthplace, spawn, and then die without ever meeting their young. It's the cycle of life. When you're standing on the banks of a river watching salmon swim upstream, it is just extraordinary. It's like watching a race from the sidelines when you see all these cyclists or runners whiz by, working incredibly hard to complete the distance. It's noisy; it's loud; it's alive. The summer-run fish should be left well alone so they can reach their final destination and spawn.

Almost all fisheries for steelhead are catch-and-release recreational fisheries, so the only choice for responsibly harvested steelhead sold commercially on the Pacific coast is farmed.

Around half of the seafood we consumed globally in 2016 was farmed—responsible aquaculture is an incredibly important resource for affordable seafood. I do support those salmon farms getting it right today with land-based recirculating systems and their continued effort to improve the way we're farming fish. Take Kuterra salmon: it's actually an Atlantic species, but it's farmed in a contained system in BC, and it holds its own flavorwise alongside the wild species.

Steelhead

Chum

Coho

• • • CATCH OF THE DAY • • •

There are five wild Pacific salmon species, each with their own distinctive qualities. Chinook—or spring—salmon is the first of the season. As the largest species, it's sometimes called king salmon; it's just this gorgeous, flavorful orangey-red fish—the big sexy beast of the salmon species. Chum (Keta) is tasty if very fresh, but it's generally cheaper and less structured than the other species and often ends up smoked. Coho salmon—also known as silver or white salmon—is a fantastic fish with mild flavor, medium fat content, and a rich reddish-orange color. Possibly the least prized Pacific salmon, pink salmon is quite soft and perishable. It's the smallest of the five species too. But chefs who care about the oceans will champion pink salmon because it is abundant. It's a great choice for salmon cakes and also inexpensive. With its terrific density, fat, and richness, sockeye is the most versatile species. Any salmon species would make a rich addition to paella (page 90), and the three firmer ones—Chinook, coho, and sockeye—would be wonderful in my Wild Salmon Bake (page 89).

Farmed Kuterra salmon and steelhead both have a great structure and mild flavor, and I enjoy using them in dishes with other flavorful ingredients such as kale, cranberries, and apples (page 78), doing them in a rich sweet-and-savory glaze of red miso and maple (page 96), and cooking them *en papillote* (page 95).

• • • PREP IT LIKE YOU OWN IT • • •

You can fillet any salmon species—they all have the same bone structure—by first removing the center bones and then the pin bones. Cut it into steaks by running a supersharp knife down the middle of the fish. Having a great set of knives is incredibly important when it comes to seafood. Sharpen yours regularly. An 8- or 10-inch chef's knife is your generic tool for cutting larger pieces of fish; an 8-inch fillet knife is good for filleting (it's a little flexible to work around the bones). And a flexible 12-inch fillet knife is good for more delicate work such as removing the skin.

●

SARDINES

RECIPES *pages 97 to 99*

• • • A FISH TALE • • •

I have great childhood memories of eating sardines simply grilled on the BBQ. My dad did all the grilling on charcoal, and he was a master of this dish. No small feat—there is just one minute between gorgeously caramelized and burnt for this oily fish. Pacific sardines are incredibly rich, and they have a distinctive fishy smell. If you weren't raised on them—as many kids outside of North America's coastal communities are not—they take some getting used to. But in places like Britain and Spain, sardines on toast is the ultimate comfort food. I say give these pretty little silver fish a second chance.

• • • A SUSTAINABILITY STORY • • •

Sardines are sensitive to environmental changes such as the water temperature rising or falling. The Pacific sardines are something of a scientific mystery because stocks go through boom-and-bust cycles. These may be caused by fluctuations of sea surface temperatures, as occur during the El Niño phenomenon.

• • • CATCH OF THE DAY • • •

While we humans either love or hate sardines, they are basically dinner to almost every creature in the ocean—they're so fatty and nourishing. You can buy them canned for convenience, but they taste spectacular fresh—a little less fishy and intense. I recommend eating the tiny bones; anything cooked on the bone has more intense flavor. And embrace the fat! Fat in fish means flavor, not unlike marbling in beef. I love sardines cured, smoked, and brined. Some acidity, from lemon or tomatoes, helps cut through their fattiness.

• • • PREP IT LIKE YOU OWN IT • • •

Leave the sardines' heads on for extra flavor, and gently rub their skin with a fish scaler to remove excess scales. Soak the fish for 10 to 15 minutes in a salt-sugar-citrus-and-spice brine to add some flavor, seal in the juices, and temper the fishy aroma.

Pacific/
Qualicum Beach

PACIFIC/QUALICUM BEACH
P. caurinus x yessoensis

WEATHERVANE
Patinopecten caurinus

PINK
Chlamys rubida

●

SCALLOPS

RECIPES *pages 147 to 151*

• • • A FISH TALE • • •

There's a winery called Sea Star in the Gulf Islands in BC whose vineyards slope down to the Pacific. At the Gold Medal Plates cooking contest in Victoria, I paired my dish with one of their white wines and drew inspiration from the dramatic setting and the sea creatures you'd find in nearby waters. The centerpiece was plump and creamy scallops and grated bottarga (scallop roe), and I arranged oysters, mussels, sidestripe shrimp, and clams alongside them to look like the shoreline. I added crabapple butter and an oyster and mussel liquor froth, whose aroma evoked the ocean. To finish: miniature lime and cucumber meringues, like puffs of cloud. This dish was so elaborate and tasty, but do you want to know a secret? My absolute favorite way to eat scallops is simply seared with a squeeze of lemon.

• • • A SUSTAINABILITY STORY • • •

In 2014, 10 million scallops died in the ocean near Qualicum Beach, BC. They couldn't form hard shells because of ocean acidification—the result of our vehicles, factories, and power plants releasing too much carbon dioxide. It was devastating. We can reduce our carbon footprint and lobby our leaders for clean energy, to protect sea creatures and plants.

• • • CATCH OF THE DAY • • •

Scallops, unlike other bivalves, are terrific swimmers; they rapidly open and shut their shells and shoot through the water, as if jet-propelled. I enjoy their sweet white meat *and* the roe; there's a frilly protective layer of orange inside the shell to which the amber eggs are attached. Cultured Pacific scallops (see left)—also known as Qualicum Beach scallops—have a firm texture and sweet, delicate flavor, making them incredibly versatile. My favorite scallops are the wild Alaskan species Weathervanes, which are relatively large and satisfying. Pink scallops are beautiful too: they're smaller and sweeter, and the shells have a rosy blush on the exterior.

My scallop recipes span the full citrus spectrum. Try this shellfish in a salad with lime pickle (page 147), roasted with grapefruit, brown butter, and thyme (page 151), or in a crudo (page 148).

• • • PREP IT LIKE YOU OWN IT • • •

Gently prize open the fan-shaped shell, and then hold it open a quarter inch and run the blade of a butter knife around it to start releasing the meat. Once the scallop is awoken, the hinge of its shell pops right open, and you can complete the job with ease.

Bull kelp

Winged kelp

Dulce

BULL KELP
Nereocystis luetkeana

WINGED KELP
Alaria esculenta

DULSE
Palmaria palmata

●

SEA GREENS

RECIPES *pages 169 to 175*

• • • A FISH TALE • • •

At Monterey Bay, in California, there's an underwater canyon twice as deep as the Grand Canyon, where the upwelling—rising of cold, algae-rich water from the bottom to the surface of the ocean—is awe-inspiring. Monterey Bay Seaweed Company drew from this source to fill their recirculating tanks, where dulse, sea lettuce, and ogo plants sway in the bubbly water. This young company sells seaweeds packaged in seawater, fresh, raw, and live, to chefs. Now that North Americans are embracing seaweed as an alternative to land-raised vegetables, I hope more such enterprises will pop up all along the Pacific coast.

• • • A SUSTAINABILITY STORY • • •

The conversation around seaweed is exciting, as we seek new ways to improve our food systems and feed our growing world population. The brainchild of Newfoundlander Bren Smith, GreenWave's "3-D ocean farms" produce mussels, oysters, scallops, and kelp in vertical columns, all in the same marine environment. Everything works together to create a healthy and resilient ecosystem, including the seaweed that can mitigate storm damage and prevent dead zones in the ocean. The earliest GreenWave ocean farms were all on the Atlantic coast, so I'm excited about the first Pacific one launching in California. PharmerSea grows seaweeds, both for the plate and for skincare products.

• • • CATCH OF THE DAY • • •

Readily available on the Pacific coast, bull kelp has ribbon-like strands that can grow to 80 feet. You can buy it fresh or dried in sheets, and it's the source of 11 vitamins and 46 minerals, not to mention amino acids, the building blocks of protein. My Kelp and Smoked Sea Salt Scones with Serrano Butter (page 172) make an extra savory and briny alternative to typical breadbasket fare. And my (Sea)Weed Brownies (page 175) hit a high note at the end of a meal. More commonly consumed species, such as nori, wakame, sugar kelp, and dulse, can be bought dried at specialty and health food stores.

• • • PREP IT LIKE YOU OWN IT • • •

To remove grittiness and beach insects, rinse foraged seaweed thoroughly 3 times in fresh cold water.

SEA URCHIN

RECIPES *pages 152 to 154*

• • • A FISH TALE • • •

My first experience of sea urchin was at the hands of Chef Yoshi Maniwa when I was 16 (living in Vancouver). My high school girlfriend and I were on the hunt for sushi, when we stumbled upon his place, Shijo. Yoshi took a shine to us kids, and he let us sample all these Japanese seafood delicacies, such as monkfish liver, mountain potato, and *uni* (sea urchin by its Japanese sushi name). There was an uni custard that I remember specifically, and it was like nothing I'd ever tasted before: it smelled and tasted like the ocean, and at the same time, it was luscious and rich—like a warm and briny crème brûlée. I still eat Yoshi's food to this day at his current restaurant, Zest, and he continues to inspire me and introduce me to exciting new ingredients.

• • • A SUSTAINABILITY STORY • • •

Second-generation fishmonger Jenice Yu has made it her mission to help Vancouverites develop a taste for indigenous species, which are prized overseas and typically exported before we have the chance to buy them. I get diver-caught sea urchins from her sustainable seafood store, F.I.S.H. (Fresh Ideas Start Here). Every town has vendors like Jenice, committed to local products. By supporting these entrepreneurs, we can boost our local economy and show some love for our planet.

• • • CATCH OF THE DAY • • •

Spiny baseball-size sea urchins are echinoderms—like starfish—with five self-sharpening teeth for biting through rocks. Sea urchins taste like creamy ocean and practically dissolve in your mouth; their sensuous flavor and texture are unlike anything else.

Sea urchins add complex and luxurious flavor to butter- and cream-based sauces. I also love them fresh and raw nigiri style, or as a salty accent to blander fish and shellfish.

• • • PREP IT LIKE YOU OWN IT • • •

One sea urchin contains about 5 uni, which is the only edible part of the shellfish. Although it's referred to as roe, it's really the reproductive organs. You can buy trays of uni from well-stocked fishmongers or order it from online retailers. You can also buy the whole urchin and remove the uni yourself. With the mouth side up, use a sharp pair of scissors to cut a large circle out of the shell. Remove the piece of shell. Dump out the seawater inside. In a mixing bowl, combine 2 cups cold water and 2 tablespoons of salt. Scoop out the uni with a spoon and place in the salty water to wash off the debris (don't leave them in the water longer than 5 minutes). Transfer to a paper-towel-lined plate to drain off the excess moisture. Cleaned uni will keep refrigerated for up to 3 days.

Spot Prawns

Sidestripe

Pacific Pink

Humpback

HUMPBACK
Pandalus hypsinotus

PACIFIC PINK/BAY/OREGON
Pandalus jordani

SPOT PRAWNS
Pandalus platyceros

SIDESTRIPE
Pandalopsis dispar

●

SHRIMP

RECIPES *pages 155 to 162*

• • • A FISH TALE • • •

There's such a buzz on Fishermen's Wharf in Vancouver, during the Spot Prawn Festival, as people of all ages line up to get their hands on a bag of spotties sold right off the boat. Families and groups of friends also sit by the water eating these beauties steamed and served with salad and warm, crusty bread. And cooking enthusiasts watch the city's best chefs take the stage to give demos.

This late-spring event was created over a decade ago to get locals excited about a local delicacy that used to be automatically shipped overseas. The city's culinary students are invited to help prepare the feast. It's crucial to get this younger generation educated about sustainable seafood and attuned to the good feelings it inspires in diners.

• • • A SUSTAINABILITY STORY • • •

In parts of Southeast Asia, unpaid workers, including children, work 16-hour days in the shrimp industry. And a fifth of the world's mangroves have been cleared for shrimp farming. These trees and shrubs growing in salty marshes are essential habitat to many coastal birds and creatures. When you invest instead in Pacific shrimp, either from recirculating aquaculture systems or well-managed wild fisheries, you are making a sustainable choice that's better for people and the planet.

• • • CATCH OF THE DAY • • •

Available fresh four to seven weeks in May and June, spot prawns are pink, spotted, and relatively large. I love them raw with a splash of soy sauce or a side of lemon aioli (page 35) for dipping. They taste sweet and mellow after a stint in the hot skillet (page 155) and bright in ceviche (page 158).

Humpback (or king) shrimp are a little smaller and have arched backs. They're beautiful raw or quickly poached in court bouillon.

Sidestripes are sweet and firm, with a distinctive stripe on their sides as their name suggests. Try them in a pasta dish with garlic confit, peas, and chili (page 161) or in a risotto (page 162).

You get around 250 to 400 Pacific pink shrimp per pound. These little sweeties are usually processed and cooked or frozen. They lend themselves well to sandwiches and rolls (page 159), especially slathered in homemade mayo, and are also star ingredients in my take on the Caesar salad (page 157).

• • • PREP IT LIKE YOU OWN IT • • •

More than other Pacific shrimp species, spot prawns can become gray and mushy if you don't use them fast. Either pull off their heads before refrigerating them fresh to prevent this or buy them frozen in seawater, which actually enhances their structure.

SKATE

RECIPES *pages 61 to 63*

• • • A FISH TALE • • •

Big Skate are like these long-tailed, majestic winged birds flapping their wings to swim through the ocean. So neat! Big skate is basically what you'd get if you flattened a shark: they're both in the elasmobranch family—alongside rays and sawfish—so their skeletons consist of soft and flexible cartilage rather than bones, and they have several rows of self-replenishing teeth.

• • • A SUSTAINABILITY STORY • • •

There are about 280 species of skate and ray around the world. Not all are sustainable. The big skate caught by bottom trawl and bottom longline in BC as part of the multispecies groundfish fisheries is a good option at this time. These fisheries are well regulated to protect corals, sponges, and rockfish conservation areas. There have been reports of unscrupulous types punching holes in a skate wing to pass off as scallops. Buying fish tagged for traceability or from a trusted vendor or community-supported fishery (CSF) offers some protection against fish fraud.

• • • CATCH OF THE DAY • • •

We eat the wings of big skate. The biggest big skate on record spanned eight feet, so as you can imagine, you have to cut those wings into manageable pieces. Visually big skate is awesome in a dish: the ridges give it a fun rippled texture with the added bonus that they let juices pool and they trap finely chopped ingredients.

Cooked gently, big skate is tender and silky, something like halibut cheeks, lobster, or sablefish. You can eat it marinated, grilled, roasted, pan-seared, or boiled. I love it with the warm umami flavors of a Japanese-inspired mushroom, sake, and ginger broth (page 63). This substantial fish also balances well with grains, such as farro (page 61), brown rice, or barley.

• • • PREP IT LIKE YOU OWN IT • • •

Buy skate wing cleaned and cut into 4- to 5-ounce square or rectangular portions. It's best to cut it against the grain to maintain tenderness. If you do happen to buy it on the bone, roast it bone-in to harness the extra flavor that will be released from the bones through cooking.

SQUID

RECIPES *pages 163 to 165*

• • • A FISH TALE • • •

When I started out at YEW, we moved away from the traditional heaping plate of crispy fried calamari and committed to offering more sustainable albeit less familiar Pacific squid species in ocean-respecting portion sizes. I'd typically pair these squid with halibut—an extremely popular fish. That gave diners a sense of security while nudging them into trying something new.

• • • A SUSTAINABILITY STORY • • •

While Humboldt squid—a jumbo cephalopod that can flash red and fly—is currently considered the most sustainable Pacific squid option, it can be difficult to find in grocery stores. As a widely accessible alternative, I recommend California Market squid. It has a life span of just around nine months, which means it repopulates fast. And there's little bycatch associated with this fishery. There's still work to do monitoring population sizes independently, so my approach is to enjoy this species as an occasional treat.

• • • CATCH OF THE DAY • • •

Small and pretty, with a speckled milky-purple shimmer, California Market squid swim wild in great big schools. These critters can change color to camouflage themselves or communicate with one another. They can grow up to about 11 inches. Fishers lure them to the surface with bright lights before netting them.

You can marinate this affordable and versatile species in buttermilk for extra tenderness, but it's not essential, as would be the case for larger (and tougher) squid. California Market squid can be bought fresh or frozen and whole or already broken down into rings, tubes, and tentacles.

This little squid makes a satisfying addition to a rich herb-infused ragout (page 164). Coated with cornmeal, crisped up, and served with a spicy mayonnaise, it can be the main event in a Mexican-style salad (page 163).

• • • PREP IT LIKE YOU OWN IT • • •

You need to be thorough when you're cleaning these little creatures: run them under cold water and pull the tentacles from the body. Then remove the beak (the hard little mouth), and be sure to slip your fingers right into the pouch and pull out all the innards and cartilage. The thin skin layer on the body should rub away easily at the end.

STURGEON

RECIPES *pages 64 to 67*

• • • A FISH TALE • • •

Some say there's a monster called Ogopogo living in Lake Okanagan. As a boy born in the Okanagan Valley, I was so scared of Ogopogo tickling my toes under the water that it actually helped me keep my balance when I was learning to water-ski. One theory is that Ogopogo is a giant sturgeon. That makes sense to me now. Survivors of the Ice Age, these plate-headed fish are impressive beasts.

• • • A SUSTAINABILITY STORY • • •

Canadian Paralympian and philanthropist Rick Hansen—aka Man in Motion—works hard alongside educators, fishers, First Nations elders, and politicians to protect white sturgeon through his foundation the Fraser River Conservation Society. It's a protected species in BC and heavily regulated in Washington State, Oregon, and California because of two centuries of overfishing to cater to our ever-growing caviar tastes. Farmed sturgeon on the Sunshine Coast is the only kind I buy: I love Northern Divine, the white sturgeon and roe farmed in Sechelt, British Columbia.

• • • CATCH OF THE DAY • • •

Sturgeon can live as long as a hundred years and grow as long as 18 feet, and you need some skill to cook it. This fish is dense, so it has to be cooked right through for a relatively long cooking time. If you overdo it, you lose the tenderness. And undercooked or raw sturgeon is almost inedible. I like this fish baked, roasted, or pan-seared. For cold preparations, I love it smoked or cured.

Because it's so full-flavored, sturgeon is best with bolder-tasting ingredients, such as caramelized onions, confit tomatoes, and capers (page 64). I think of it as a fall and winter fish, for when you're craving rich and soothing foods. Oven-baked sturgeon with lentils and watercress is a wonderfully comforting dish (page 66).

I like to treat the roe—caviar—as simply as possible. I'll serve it chilled and naked, or in a surf-and-surf dish, such as pan-seared scallops with caviar crème fraîche or caviar butter with spot prawns. Beautiful!

• • • PREP IT LIKE YOU OWN IT • • •

Since sturgeon is naturally boneless—it has cartilage, like sharks—you don't need to worry about deboning it. Just ask your fishmonger to cut it into 4- to 5-ounce portions, one per person.

TUNA

RECIPES *pages 100 to 105*

• • • A FISH TALE • • •

I sometimes see people posing proudly with freshly caught bluefin tuna on social media, but I'd be happier if we all just left those fish in the ocean. Yes, they're awe-inspiring creatures, but they're also the poster child of overfished predator species. Diners crave bluefin for its steak-like qualities, but we need to be as upset about huge tuna disappearing from the oceans as we are about lions and tigers disappearing from the jungle.

• • • A SUSTAINABILITY STORY • • •

Fortunately, we can buy albacore tuna as a responsible tuna alternative. It's smaller, at a market size of 10 to 40 pounds as opposed to an average of 550 pounds for Atlantic bluefin; it comes to maturity faster; and it reproduces frequently, from the tender age of five—all of which is great for sustainability. You can't sub it into many yellowfin or bluefin dishes because those other bigger tunas are often served in big steak-like pieces. But we need to stop thinking of tuna in steak terms anyway—it's time to use it more sparingly, as an accent, and make it matter.

• • • CATCH OF THE DAY • • •

Cut into a gorgeous loin of albacore tuna, and the fat will glisten on your knife. One of my top 10 fish. It's incredibly rich, so it lends itself well to raw preparations, such as tartare or crudo. This fish freezes well too and is sold in loins, so it's supereasy to use.

It's excellent lightly dressed in crudo (page 100) or with a richer tahini, lemon, and honey dressing as tataki (page 103). I also enjoy it in a poke (page 101). And the canned version is what you need for a creamy, artichoke-enhanced tuna melt (page 104).

• • • PREP IT LIKE YOU OWN IT • • •

Albacore tuna is typically sold frozen, in large loins, so you need to trim it down for pan-frying. I recommend asking your fishmonger to take care of it—that's what they do best—as it can be a little fiddly. If you're doing it yourself, simply slice the edges off the top and bottom of the loin, then slice off the belly and reserve it for a delicious tuna tartare.

METRIC CONVERSION CHART

VOLUME

Imperial	Metric
⅛ tsp	0.5 mL
¼ tsp	1 mL
½ tsp	2.5 mL
¾ tsp	4 mL
1 tsp	5 mL
½ Tbsp	8 mL
1 Tbsp	15 mL
1½ Tbsp	23 mL
2 Tbsp	30 mL
¼ cup	60 mL
⅓ cup	80 mL
½ cup	125 mL
⅔ cup	165 mL
¾ cup	185 mL
1 cup	250 mL
1¼ cups	310 mL
1⅓ cups	330 mL
1½ cups	375 mL
1⅔ cups	415 mL
1¾ cups	435 mL
2 cups	500 mL
2¼ cups	560 mL
2⅓ cups	580 mL
2½ cups	625 mL
2¾ cups	690 mL
3 cups	750 mL
4 cups / 1 qt	1 L
5 cups	1.25 L
6 cups	1.5 L
7 cups	1.75 L
8 cups / 2 qts	2 L
10 cups	2.5 L
3 quarts	3 L
4 quarts	4 L
5 quarts	5 L

WEIGHT

Imperial	Metric
1 oz	30 g
2 oz	60 g
3 oz	85 g
4 oz (¼ lb)	115 g
5 oz	140 g
6 oz	170 g
7 oz	200 g
8 oz (½ lb)	225 g
9 oz	255 g
10 oz	285 g
11 oz	310 g
12 oz (¾ lb)	340 g
13 oz	370 g
14 oz	400 g
15 oz	425 g
1 lb (16 oz)	450 g
1½ lb	670 g
2 lb	900 g
3 lb	1.4 kg
4 lb	1.8 kg
5 lb	2.3 kg
6 lb	2.7 kg
12 lb	5.4 kg

CANS

Imperial	Metric
5 oz	140 g
15 oz	425 g

LINEAR

Imperial	Metric
⅛ inch	3 mm
¼ inch	6 mm
½ inch	12 mm
¾ inch	2 cm
1 inch	2.5 cm
1½ inches	3.5 cm
2 inches	5 cm
3 inches	7.5 cm
4 inches	10 cm
5 inches	12.5 cm
6 inches	15 cm
7 inches	18 cm
8 inches	20 cm
9 inches	23 cm
10 inches	25 cm
11 inches	28 cm
12 inches (1 foot)	30 cm
18 inches	46 cm

OVEN TEMPERATURE

Imperial	Metric
200°F	95°C
250°F	120°C
275°F	135°C
300°F	150°C
325°F	160°C
350°F	180°C
375°F	190°C
400°F	200°C
425°F	220°C
450°F	230°C
475°F	240°C
500°F	260°C

TEMPERATURE

Imperial	Metric
120°F	49°C
125°F	52°C
130°F	54°C
140°F	60°C
150°F	66°C
160°F	71°C
170°F	77°C
180°F	82°C
190°F	88°C
200°F	93°C
250°F	121°C
300°F	149°C
325°F	163°C
340°F	171°C
350°F	177°C
360°F	182°C
375°F	191°C

RESOURCES

CANADA

BRITISH COLUMBIA

Haida Gwaii

North Pacific Kelp
northpacifickelp.com

Vancouver

Dock to Dish
docktodish.com

Fanny Bay Oysters
fannybayoysters.com

The Fish Counter
thefishcounter.com

Fresh Ideas Start Here
eatfish.ca

Nextjen (gluten-free flours)
nextjen.ca

Organic Ocean
organicocean.com

Skipper Otto's Community
Supported Fishery
skipperotto.com

Walter (craft Caesar mix)
waltercaesar.com

Vancouver Island

Canadian Kelp Resources
canadiankelp.com

Dakini Tidal Wilds
dakinitidalwilds.com

Out Landish Shellfish Guild
outlandish-shellfish.com

Vancouver Island Salt Co.
visaltco.com

UNITED STATES

ALASKA

Anchorage

FishEx
fishex.com

Juneau

Alaska Glacier Seafoods
alaskaglacierseafoods.com

Alaska Seafood Marketing
Institute
alaskaseafood.org

Hooked Seafood Company
Alaska
hookedseafoods.com

Taku River Reds
taku-salmon.com

Taku Fisheries
takustore.com

CALIFORNIA

Bay Area

Hudson Fish Company
hudsonfish.com

Monterey Fish Market
montereyfish.com

Los Angeles

Chesapeake Fish Co.
santamonicaseafood.com

Dory Fleet
doryfleet.com

Mitsuwa Marketplace
mitsuwa.com

Santa Monica Seafood
santamonicaseafood.com

Wild Local Seafood Co.
wildlocalseafood.com

Monterey and Santa Cruz

H&H Fresh Fish Co.
hhfreshfish.com

Monterey Bay Seaweeds
montereybayseaweeds.com

Phil's Fish Market
philsfishmarket.com

Robbie's Ocean Fresh
Seafood
(no website)

San Diego

Catalina Offshore Products
catalinaop.com

San Francisco

Four Star Seafood
fourstarseafood.com

TwoXSea
twoxsea.com

Water2Table Fish Co.
water2table.com

OREGON

South Beach

South Beach Fish Market
southbeachfishmarket.com

Portland

New Seasons Market
newseasonsmarket.com

Newman's Fish Company
newmansfish.com

Pacific Seafood
pacseafood.com

True World Foods
trueworldfoods.com

WASHINGTON

Seattle

Lam's Seafood Market
lamsseafood.com

Mutual Fish Company
mutualfish.com

Pike Place Fish Market
pikeplacefish.com

Pure Food Fish Market
freshseafood.com

Taylor Shellfish Farms
taylorshellfishfarms.com

ACKNOWLEDGMENTS

FIRST AND FOREMOST, THANK YOU TO MY LIFE PARTNER AND WIFE, KATE COLLEY. Thanks for supporting my dreams, even when it has not been easy. You are a wonderful mother to our sons, and have been my rock as I've worked on this book and mission of mine. Thanks for amplifying the message of Chefs for Oceans through your amazing company, Colley Communications. You are a PR and marketing dynamo. Our home is where my heart is.

Thanks to my coauthor, Valerie Howes, for helping me transform my thoughts and ideas into beautiful prose. You were an early Chefs for Oceans supporter, and I appreciate all the work you do as a journalist telling stories that shine a spotlight on food security.

I'm incredibly grateful to Chris Labonté, our publisher, for instantly recognizing the value in a sustainable-seafood cookbook. You and the Figure 1 team have worked so hard to make this book both an invaluable resource and a visual feast for home cooks. To Michelle Meade, our incisive editor, thank you for your vision: you opened my eyes to the possibilities of covering the entire Pacific coast and took this project to the next level.

I was moved by the astonishingly smooth—I'd go as far as to say magical—creative process behind the visuals in this book. Thank you to our photographer, Kevin Clark—you are a master of light—and to our tremendously talented illustrator,

Dale Nigel Goble. I'm infinitely grateful to our stylist, Lawren Moneta, who worked so hard to prep the food for our shoots (then graciously let me swoop in at the end and steal the credit). And I bow down to our designer, Jessica Sullivan—you have extraordinary creative talents and you really made the images sing with your ability to start from two thousand feet above the project then hone in on the tiniest details. A special shout-out to my best friend Jed Grieve and the Cook Culture teams (cookculture.com), who supported this book from start to finish and lent us their studio space for the shoot.

Lana Brandt, my friend and Chefs for Oceans project manager and the former national SeaChoice manager; and Ann-Marie Copping, the manager of Vancouver Aquarium's Ocean Wise sustainable seafood program, you've been my left and right hands for the past 10 years. Thanks for all you've done to educate and challenge me, breaking things down whenever I've picked up the phone to ask about a species, catch method, or aspect of the human conversation around the fishing industry.

I'm also indebted to Claire Li Loong, Teddie Geach, Deirdre Finn, Tania Leon, Laurenne Schiller, and Isabella Sulpizio and all the Ocean Wise partners and ambassadors across Canada. You do remarkable work inspiring chefs and diners. Sheila Bowman (Seafood Watch manager of culinary and strategic initiatives), you've been my guiding light in understanding sustainable seafood in the United States and inviting me into the circle of my peers with the Blue Ribbon Task Force and Cooking for Solutions. I'm also indebted to my friends at the Marine Stewardship Council (MSC), World Wildlife Fund (WWF), and Oceana. With so many voices calling for ocean conservation, traceability, chain of custody, and seafood protection, we have a solid chance of making a difference.

In the world of fish, I have many mentors, but it all started with Chef Rob Clark. You shifted my perspective and kick-started my conscience when I was a young chef. And in cofounding the Ocean Wise sustainable seafood program with another one of my heroes, marine biologist–turned–fishmonger Mike McDermid, you created a sea change across the supply chain, from fisher to chef to table. Thank you also to culinary giants Rick Moonen, Barton Seaver, Michael Cimarusti, and Dan Barber. You are legends and a constant source of inspiration for all of us across North America. Thank you for cooking with me, to raise awareness around the ethics of seafood, and for welcoming me into your worlds.

To Terroir founder, Arlene Stein, Rebecca Mackenzie, Renee Lalonde, Voula Halliday, Valerie Howes, Michelle Cyr, and all committee members past and present, thank you for creating a forum for vital debate and discussion around the big restaurant-industry issues of our times. Above all, thanks for spearheading the One Fish mission to St. John's, Newfoundland. It gave me new perspectives on Canadian fisheries and underlined that when we speak up together, we can influence our peers and the politicians to bring about meaningful change.

Thank you for your generous support to all the friends and supporters of Chefs for Oceans; to Vancity; to Tony Allard and the Wild Salmon Forever family; and to Christina Burridge, Sandra Merk, and all our partners and the fishers of BC Seafood Alliance.

Every day, I am inspired by the fishers who risk their lives on the water to bring wild seafood to our plates. I'm also tremendously respectful of those pioneers in aquaculture, creating responsible farming systems to help feed a growing world population, set to hit nine billion by the year 2050. There are so many to thank, but I'd like to make a special shout-out to a few dear friends: Steve Johansen, Frank Keitsch, and Dane Chauvel from Organic Ocean; Otto, Shaun, and Sonia Strobel from Skipper Otto; and Stewart McDonald, my favorite lone wolf of the high seas. Keep catching the fish; I'll keep making it delicious. What a gift and a privilege to still be able to eat wild seafood—let's never lose sight of that.

INDEX

ABOUT THE AUTHORS

NED BELL founded Chefs for Oceans in 2014 to raise awareness and advocate for responsible seafood choices and to highlight the importance of healthy oceans, lakes, and rivers. The West Coast seafood ambassador defines his cuisine as globally inspired, locally created, and plant-based. Ned was executive chef of Four Seasons Hotel Vancouver and YEW seafood + bar until 2016, when he became the Ocean Wise Executive Chef. Ned is currently a member of Seafood Watch's Blue Ribbon Task Force. He was named Canada's Chef of the Year at the Pinnacle Awards in 2014, honored with the 2015 Green Award for Sustainability by *Vancouver* magazine, and, most recently, awarded 2017 Seafood Champion for Advocacy by SeaWeb Seafood. As the father of three incredible sons, he is dedicated to inspiring everybody who cooks or eats fish to become part of the solution so that future generations can enjoy ocean-friendly catch.

VALERIE HOWES grew up just across the water from Edinburgh in Fife, a Scottish county on the east coast, where fishing villages and working harbors dot the coastline. Today, she lives with her family in Toronto, always a little nostalgic for the sound of the sea. As the food editor of *Reader's Digest* Canada, Valerie created a blog about Canadian food culture, *Open Kitchen.* It won Gold for Best Blog at the Canadian Society of Magazine Editors Awards and the Canadian Online Publishing Awards, as well as a National Magazine Awards nomination. Valerie has written about culinary travel, sustainable food systems, and people who're making a difference in their communities, for publications such as *enRoute*, Martha Stewart's *Whole Living*, *Globe and Mail*, *National Post*, *Canadian Living*, *Chatelaine*, *Pure Canada,* and *Today's Parent.* Her next book project explores the edible landscapes and seascapes of Fogo Island, Newfoundland.

CHEFS FOR **OCEANS**